WAITING FOR GODOT

_____ *form in*

movement _____

TWAYNE'S MASTERWORK STUDIES
ROBERT LECKER, GENERAL EDITOR

WAITING FOR GODOT

_____ *form in*
movement _____

Thomas Cousineau

TWAYNE PUBLISHERS

A Division of G. K. Hall & Co.

To my mother and father

Waiting for Godot: form in movement
Thomas Cousineau

Twayne's Masterwork Studies No. 33

Copyright 1990 by G. K. Hall & Co.
All rights reserved
Published by Twayne Publishers
A Division of G. K. Hall & Co.
70 Lincoln Street
Boston, MA 02111

Production photos are by Jacqueline Yves Lifton from the 1988
television production "Beckett Directs Beckett" by Cameras
Continentales, Paris, and the Visual Press, University of Maryland,
College Park. Rufus plays Vladimir; Jean-François Balmer, Estragon;
Jean-Pierre Jorris, Pozzo; and Roman Polanski, Lucky.

Book production and design by John Amburg
Copyediting supervised by Barbara Sutton
Typeset in 10/14 Sabon
by Huron Valley Graphics, Ann Arbor, Michigan

Printed on permanent/durable acid-free paper
and bound in the United States of America

Library of Congress Cataloging-in-Publication Data

Cousineau, Thomas.
    Waiting for Godot : form in movement / Thomas Cousineau.
        p.   cm.—(Twayne's masterwork studies ; no. 33)
    Bibliography: p.
    Includes index.
    ISBN 0-8057-7974-4 (alk. paper).—ISBN 0-8057-8024-6 (pbk. :
alk. paper)
    1. Beckett, Samuel, 1906–   En attendant Godot.   I. Title.
II. Series.
PQ2603.E378E636   1990
842'.914–dc20

89-15504
CIP

CONTENTS

Note on the References and Acknowledgments
Chronology: Samuel Beckett's Life and Works

1. Historical Context		1
2. The Importance of the Work		6
3. Critical Reception		10

A Reading

4. Introduction		21
5. Christianity		25
6. Truth		32
7. Language		43
8. Causality		53
9. Memory and Expectation		62
10. Friendship		71
11. Family		79
12. Visual Form		89
13. Metaphor and Metonymy		97
14. Repetition and Difference		105
15. Metatheater		117

Notes	127
Bibliography	130
Index	134
About the Author	136

Note on the References
and Acknowledgments

All references to *Waiting for Godot* are to Beckett's translation (New York: Grove Press, 1954), which is based on the original edition of the play, *En Attendant Godot* (Paris: Editions de Minuit, 1952). For details of staging I refer frequently to Beckett's 1975 production of *Godot* at the Schiller Theater in Berlin, videotapes of which were lent to me by Dougald McMillan and Walter Asmus. I am also deeply grateful to James Knowlson, founder and curator of the Beckett Archives at the University of Reading, for allowing me to consult Beckett's notebooks for this production. English and French versions of *Godot*, directed by Beckett in 1988 and closely resembling his earlier staging of the play, have been produced by the Visual Press of the University of Maryland and Cameras Continentales, Paris, and are available on videocassette. A leave of absence and a research grant from Washington College allowed me to complete this study under exceptionally favorable circumstances.

Production photos are by Jacqueline Yves Lifton from the 1988 television production "Beckett Directs Beckett" by Cameras Continentales, Paris, and the Visual Press, University of Maryland, College Park. Rufus plays Vladimir; Jean-François Balmer, Estragon; Jean-Pierre Jorris, Pozzo; and Roman Polanski, Lucky.

SAMUEL BECKETT
Photograph by Louis Monier, used by permission.

Chronology:

SAMUEL BECKETT'S LIFE AND WORKS

1906　Samuel Beckett born on Good Friday, 13 April, in Dublin into a respectable Protestant family. Admits to a happy childhood, but with qualification that he "had little talent for happiness." Studies French as a child, but without any special interest.

1920　Sent to Portora School, one of the most prestigious Protestant boarding schools in Ireland. Shows more interest in sports, especially cricket, than in academic subjects.

1923　Enrolls in Trinity College, Dublin. Comes under the influence of Rudmose-Brown, professor of French and Italian, which becomes his special area of academic interest. Introduced to Dublin literary life; admires Sean O'Casey but prefers continental drama.

1926　First visit to France, a bicycle tour of the Loire Valley. Parents find him increasingly a "stranger in their midst." Studies German, whose precision and rigidity he admires.

1928　Graduates first in his class in modern languages from Trinity; awarded two-year teaching appointment at the École Normale Supérieure in Paris. Introduced to James Joyce's circle: "Joyce had a moral effect on me; he made me realize artistic integrity."

1929　Writes, at Joyce's urging, an essay on *Finnegans Wake*. Studies Schopenhauer and Descartes, who are to leave a lasting imprint on his work. His first short story, "Assumption," published in *transition*.

1930   His poem on Descartes and time, *Whoroscope,* wins literary prize. Commissioned to write book on Marcel Proust's novel, *Remembrance of Things Past.* Reads and admires Jules Renard because "He always speaks so well about chewing and pissing and that kind of thing." Awarded appointment to the faculty at Trinity College but dislikes teaching intensely: "I did not enjoy all those women mooning about." Confinement in Ireland leads to psychosomatic illnesses, which will be alleviated only by return to Paris.

1931   Begins writing an unfinished novel, *Dream of Fair to Middling Women.*

1933   Life in Dublin complicated by illness and difficulty of deciding on a life's work. Death of Peggy Sinclair, a cousin to whom he had once been romantically attached. Father dies of a heart attack. Turned down for a position as assistant curator at the National Gallery. Considers going to Russia to study cinema with Sergei Eisenstein, who does not, however, reply to letter offering his services.

1934   Publishes a collection of short stories, *More Pricks Than Kicks;* no public success, but admired by Joyce. Writes many of the poems that appear in *Echoes Bones.*

1936   Considers becoming a commercial airline pilot: "I do not feel like spending the rest of my life writing books that no one will read. It was not as though I wanted to write them." Begins meeting people in Dublin theatrical world. *Murphy,* first completed novel, accepted for publication.

1937   Goes to Germany to look at paintings; notices that Nazis have removed "decadent" modern paintings from museums. Returns to Paris in the last week of October: "I came back to Paris and lived in a hotel for some time and then decided to settle down and make my life here." Hospitalized after being stabbed by an underworld character, he is visited by a young pianist whom he will later marry.

1939   On vacation in Dublin, he returns immediately to Paris after hearing of France's declaration of war against Germany.

1940   Becomes politically involved because he "was so outraged by the Nazis, particularly by their treatment of the Jews, that I could not remain inactive."

1942   Pursued by the Gestapo for his Resistance activities, he escapes with his wife to the south of France.

1945   Awarded Croix de Guerre: "A man of great courage . . . he continued his work well past the limit of personal security. Betrayed to the Germans, from 1943 he was forced to live clandestinely and with great difficulty." Writes *Mercier and Camier,* a novella containing characters and situations resembling those of *Godot.*

Chronology: Samuel Beckett's Life and Works

1946   Begins what he calls "the siege in the room," his most productive creative period, during which he will write the trilogy of novels (*Molloy, Malone Dies,* and *The Unnamable*) and *Waiting for Godot.* Surprised by words that spring directly from his unconscious, he has little memory of writing them.

1948   Writes *Waiting for Godot,* in French, from 9 October to 29 January 1949, "as a relaxation, to get away from the awful prose I was writing at the time." Finds writing for the stage a "marvelous, liberating diversion," much like playing chess.

1950   His wife brings manuscript of *Godot* to Roger Blin, who begins trying to arrange its production.

1951   Publication of *Molloy* and *Malone Dies.* Writes nothing new, devoting himself to obtaining a production for *Godot.*

1953   Opening of *Godot* on 5 January at the Théâtre de Babylone in Paris. Publication of its English translation.

1954   Begins writing *Endgame;* completed in 1956, first performed in 1957.

1955   Goes to see London production of *Godot* with Alan Schneider, who is preparing Miami opening: disturbed by clutter, lack of simplicity. Irritated by misunderstandings to which play is subjected: "Why do people have to complicate a thing so simple I can't make out."

1956   American opening of *Godot* in Miami before an audience misled by its billing as "the laugh sensation of two continents." Opens more successfully in New York.

1957   Herbert Blau directs *Godot* at San Quentin Prison; reputedly obscure and intellectual play draws perceptive and enthusiastic reviews from inmates. "All That Fall," his first radio play, broadcast on the BBC. *Act without Words I,* a mime with music by Beckett's cousin, John Beckett, performed at the Royal Court Theatre in London.

1958   *Krapp's Last Tape,* his first postwar writing in English, performed at the Royal Court Theatre.

1959   First broadcast of "Embers," a radio play, on the BBC.

1960   Writes last novel, *How It Is.* Goes to Dublin to receive an honorary degree from Trinity College.

1961   First performance of *Happy Days,* in New York.

1962   Irish actor Jack MacGowran performs one-man show *End of Day;* Beckett tells him that in cases where multiple meanings are possible, he should choose the most obvious; he is very tired of "symbol-hunting scholars" who seemed to be breathing down his neck all the time.

1963   Goes to Germany to assist production of *Play:* is so impressed by professionalism and technical perfection of director, actors, and crew that he decides to direct all of his plays that are planned for Germany. Wants to return to his important work, that is, prose fiction. Goes to the United States to help Alan Schneider with production of *Film;* finds New York less terrifying than he had expected.

1965 French production of his first television play, *Eh Joe.*

1967 Directs *Endgame* at the Schiller Theater. Will return to the same theater in 1969 to direct *Krapp's Last Tape* and in 1971 for *Happy Days.*

1969 On vacation in Tunisia, learns that he has been awarded the Nobel Prize for "a body of work that, in new forms of fiction and the theatre, has transmuted the destitution of modern man into his exaltation." Refuses to be represented in Sweden by the Irish ambassador.

1973 Rejects request from Estelle Parsons and Shelley Winters to perform in *Godot,* insisting that roles must be played by men.

1975 Begins rehearsing *Godot* at the Schiller Theater in late December. This production is both praised for choreographic precision and criticized for lack of spontaneity and vitality. Directs Pierre Chabert in *Krapp's Last Tape* and Madeleine Renaud in *Not I* at the Théâtre d'Orsay in Paris.

1979 Directs *Happy Days* at the Royal Court Theatre. Writes *A Piece of Monologue* for English actor David Warrilow; first performed in New York in 1980.

1980 Writes *Rockaby,* directed by Alan Schneider and performed by the English actress Billie Whitelaw the following year in Buffalo, New York.

1981 Writes *Ohio Impromptu,* performed the same year at a Beckett symposium sponsored by Ohio State University.

1982 *Catastrophe,* dedicated to Czech dissident playwright Vaclav Havel, performed at the Avignon Festival.

1988 Supervises production of *Godot* codirected by Walter Asmus, his assistant at the Schiller Theater, and performed by actors from the San Quentin Drama Workshop, founded by ex-convict Rick Cluchey.

1

Historical Context

Samuel Beckett arrived in Paris in 1928 with the intention of writing a scholarly work on the French poet Pierre-Jean Jouve and returning to Dublin, where an academic position awaited him at Trinity College. However, the exhilaration of finding himself in the midst of the most important artistic revolution of the twentieth century quickly put those modest ambitions to an end. He was immediately welcomed into the circle of his compatriot James Joyce, who had taken up residence in Paris several years earlier. Beckett had already read and admired Joyce's experimental novel *Ulysses* (1922), whose technical innovations would find echoes in his own work. He would soon write an article on "Work in Progress," eventually published as *Finnegans Wake* (1939), in which his praise for Joyce's rupture with traditional literature foreshadows his own radical break with the past.[1] Marcel Proust, the other twentieth-century novelist whom Beckett admired, died in 1922, but publication of his multivolume *Remembrance of Things Past* was not completed until 1927. In response to a commission for a critical study of *Remembrance*, Beckett wrote a book that is ostensibly about Proust but that also remains the best introduction to his own work.[2]

Surrealism, the most important artistic movement of the 1920s, also exerted a strong influence on Beckett. The term itself had been invented in 1917 by Guillaume Apollinaire and was adopted several years later by a group of writers and artists whose experience of the collapse of traditional values in the aftermath of World War I led them to a radical critique of the ideological foundations of Western civilization. Beckett read surrealist poetry with great enthusiasm and translated into English the work of poets belonging to the movement. His interest in surrealism was prophetic in the sense that he was eventually to write a play, *Waiting for Godot*, that would, in its turn, be widely interpreted as expressing the sense of dislocation caused by World War II.

Writers as diverse as Joyce, Proust, and the surrealist poets were united by their interest in moments of intense perception that free the self from its bondage to ordinary consciousness. They believed that personality is disfigured by the repression exerted by the waking self, which keeps us ignorant of unconscious experiences that refuse confinement within the stultifying parameters of rationality and logic.

Joyce called moments of release from ordinary consciousness "epiphanies" and used them in his first novel, *A Portrait of the Artist as a Young Man,* to create a tension between the waking thoughts and the buried, unconscious thoughts of his main character, Stephen Dedalus. Stephen's epiphanies, which rescue him from the burdensome preoccupations of daily life, are provoked by vivid concrete images, which revive suppressed infantile memories and dissipate the alienating effects of rational, adult consciousness. In Proust's novel, the power of conscious thought is likewise overthrown by the spontaneous upsurge of intense emotions in response to concrete sensations, described by the narrator as moments of "involuntary memory" because they are beyond the reach of his conscious will. His absorption in these momentary experiences liberates him from concerns about the future, including the prospect of his eventual death. These radiant instants have the further power of resurrecting his deepest self, which he had thought dead but which he now discovers to have been merely dormant.

Like Joyce and Proust, the surrealists were interested in experiences that liberate the unconscious mind from the constraints of rationality, which they similarly regarded as an obstacle to the discovery of one's true self. In the *Surrealist Manifesto* (1925), André Breton announced that the goal of this movement was to reveal the true nature of thought by rejecting any control exercised by reason and logic. To this end, the surrealists employed the techniques of automatic writing, the recording of dreams, and the inducement of such borderline mental states as hypnosis and hallucination in order to gain access to moments of "surreal" experience.

The experiments that Beckett was later to undertake in the theater are prefigured by the theories of Antonin Artaud, who was himself associated with the surrealist movement until his expulsion in 1927.[3] Essentially, Artaud applied the conflict between conscious and unconscious experience to the distinction between the verbal text of a play, which conveys its rational meanings, and the concrete scenic language created by movement and gesture, which addresses itself directly to the prerational self. Artaud felt that Western theater mistakenly emphasized the theatrical text, to which it subordinated all other expressive elements. Rather than simply illustrating or clarifying the meanings of the text, the scenic images of a play should, in Artaud's view, assert their radical autonomy from meaning. His belief that verbal language has only limited expressive powers led Artaud to see in the overthrow of this language the possibility of rediscovering much deeper forms of consciousness than those to which it allowed access.

Artaud's theoretical writings also foreshadow the extraordinary precision with which movement and gesture are calculated in Beckett's plays. Artaud praised the Balinese theater, which performed in Paris in 1930, for the exceptional precision, "the mathematical minuteness" of the presentation of ritual gestures. This quality is also found in the best productions of *Godot,* including the one directed by Beckett in 1975 at the Schiller Theater, and renders the stage image of the play even more vivid and resonant.

Since Beckett achieves in *Godot* that revolutionary return to concrete experience that he praised in Joyce and Proust and that Artaud saw as the key to the renovation of Western theater, it is appropriate that the director of the original Paris production of *Godot,* Roger Blin, should have been closely associated with Artaud. In his memoirs, Blin describes how his conception of *Godot,* with Beckett's obvious blessing, had significant affinities with Artaud's theories.[4] He underscores, for example, the concrete quality of his staging of the play and the diminished emphasis on its abstract meanings, when he refers to the "the rhythm and respiration" of *Godot.* Further, he recalls Artaud's enthusiasm for the mathematical precision of Balinese theater when he compares directing the play to choreographing a ballet, in which every detail of movement is precisely and rigorously controlled.

All of Beckett's plays are constructed around a vivid stage image: the two tramps on the country road in *Godot,* the stage that resembles the interior of a skull in *Endgame,* the characters enclosed in urns in *Play,* Winnie buried in a mound in *Happy Days,* the disembodied mouth of *Not I,* the woman in her rocking chair in *Rockaby.* This preeminence of concrete visual images becomes even more marked in his most recent plays, in which the brevity of the text allows us to focus attention almost exclusively on the scenic space of the play. Even in his prose fiction, a genre that cannot entirely dispense with language, Beckett uses words to evoke vivid images rather than to tell stories or convey meanings. Although his plays do not dispense with the text as radically as Artaud recommended, he does create a fundamental tension between text and scenic imagery, using the text to express feelings of loss and deprivation and the stage image to fix attention on the present moment and the aesthetic pleasures it offers.

Beckett once remarked that the seed of *Godot* lay in his first published novel, *Murphy,* which centers on the hero's effort to achieve momentary release from bondage to ordinary consciousness. At first glance, the liberating moments described in *Murphy* seem to have no equivalent in *Godot.* Rather than struggling to escape from alienating constraints, Vladimir and Estragon actively embrace them by awaiting the arrival of Godot. When we watch a production of the play, however, we come to a startling discovery. Those moments of release that are generally absent from the dialogue of the play are in fact continuously conveyed through its visual form. The relations between characters and props, based on the poetic figures of metaphor and metonymy, the rhythms and geometrical figures that characters produce through their movements and gestures, and the interplay of repetition and difference throughout the play bring characters little benefit but convey to us intimations of layers of experience beyond the reach of ordinary meanings. In this way, they reawaken those spontaneous sources of replenishment so valued by Beckett's precursors.

2

The Importance of the Work

W *aiting for Godot* makes severe demands on its audiences, subjecting them to unconventional theatrical practices that have left many disoriented, frustrated, bored, or angry. In spite of this, the play's power to evoke deep emotional responses in diverse groups of people has always been recognized. The most striking example of its success with audiences was the production of *Godot* presented at San Quentin Prison in 1957. The inmates responded with unexpected enthusiasm, interpreting the play as a literal image of their own incarceration. One of them, Rick Cluchey, began a correspondence with Beckett that led to their collaboration after he was released from prison. The culmination of their work together was the 1988 production of *Godot*, directed by Beckett in Paris and performed by the San Quentin Drama Workshop, with Cluchey playing the role of Pozzo.

Other spectators have been strongly affected by the play, though perhaps in less decisive fashion. Some have found in it an expression of those doubts, fears, and anxieties that arise from the sense of living in a time when traditional points of reference no longer seem valid. For these spectators, *Godot* reflects a sense of crisis and urgency that can be traced to Friedrich Nietzsche's announcement of the death of God and the existentialist themes of alienation and despair. Others have found in the play a mirror of the dehumanizing effects of modern technological societies that have, in the name of progress, left men with a curious sense of dislocation and emptiness. Still others have pointed to the master/slave dialectic dramatized by Pozzo and Lucky as a representation of social and political relationships based on exploitation. All interpretations—ethical, religious, psychological, and political—attest to the importance of *Godot* as a reflection of the most pressing concerns of contemporary audiences.

Godot's place in the history of modern theater is equally significant. Beckett's refusal to subscribe to the conventions of plot and character, his exploration of new structural principles, such as the use of repetition and difference, and his foregrounding of verbal games and non sequitur rather than "meaningful" dialogue stimulated some of the most important theatrical experiments of the past few decades. The intense experimentation that characterized fiction and poetry in the twenties was not to reach the theater until later. It is, therefore, appropriate that Beckett, who began his literary career as a novelist and poet amid the radical experiments of the earlier part of the century, should also be one of the great theatrical innovators of the modern period.

We may think of *Waiting for Godot* as the fulfillment in theatrical form of a revolution introduced into modern literature by writers who, dissatisfied with the abstractness and lack of vitality that they found in their inherited literary language, tried to revitalize language by restoring to it some of its original relationship to the concreteness of physical gesture. Beckett took this search for concreteness one step further by rejecting the traditional prejudice that the essence of a play is in the text, to which all other details of the production must be subordinated. As his 1975 Schiller Theater production of the play makes clear, the text of *Godot* is not a privileged vehicle that asserts its superiority over all other theatrical forms of expression. Rather, this text coexists with a concrete scenic language created by movement and gesture that frequently acquires its own autonomy and conveys quite different meanings. This shift in emphasis from text to movement amounts to a literary equivalent of the Copernican Revolution, in the sense that like Copernicus, who changed our perception of the relation between the sun and the earth, Beckett has, in effect, dislodged the text from its traditional prominence and placed physical movement at the center of his play.

This revolution is not limited to literary history. It reflects a much deeper shift that has been occurring over the past several centuries and whose signs are evident in social and political, as well as cultural, manifestations—that is, the questioning of the legitimacy of patriarchal society. Beckett has created in *Godot* a patriarchal world that does not work: Godot does not come and Pozzo, the paternalistic master, is, by the second act of the play, pathetically dependent on his servant. The implications of this situation are far-reaching.

Patriarchy does not consist simply in demoting matriarchal figures and replacing them with fathers. It also results in the privileging of certain activities at the expense of others; in particular, it marks a decisive shift in the relative values attached to sensual and abstract modes of perception. Sigmund Freud underlines this aspect of patriarchy in *Moses and Monotheism*. [5] As Freud points out, the prohibition against making images of God that prevailed among Old Testament Jews resulted in the compulsion to worship an invisible God, an observation in which we recognize analogies to Vladimir and Estragon's predicament. This compulsion led to the promotion of abstract ideas over sense impressions and the valorization of such categories as reason, logic, and hierarchy. In Freud's view, this victory of the intellectual over the sensual was an undoubted advantage; it constituted a great step forward for mankind because it permitted those progressive achievements through which man was able to extend his mastery over the world and improve his chances for obtaining happiness.

Godot implies that the shift to patriarchy has been a momentously wrong step. Beckett presents characters who have arguably been rendered less intelligent by their attachment to an invisible source of power and meaning. Indeed, the play would seem to defend the antipatriarchal assertion, of which Freud was not unaware, that the promotion of rationality over sensuality, whatever benefits it may provide in terms of increased mastery, actually alienates the individual subject from those creative, unconscious well-springs of life that are the only authentic sources of human happiness.

In the midst of all the time spent waiting for the arrival of Godot, no one seems to notice the absence of women on stage. The play implies, in this way, that the preoccupation with serving an alienating master leads to a loss of contact with the creative sources of life. At the same time, Beckett does offer access to the feminine through the poetry of concrete movement and gesture, which restores to the play that sensual dimension of which it had been deprived by the obsession with Godot. The mother has disappeared from the play in her person and cannot be directly revived. However, she not ony survives but asserts her superior claim to our attachment through the spatial form of the play, in which we discover immediate sensual pleasures of whose existence characters on stage seem to have little inkling.

3

Critical Reception

The popular success of *Waiting for Godot* must be one of the most improbable events in theatrical history. Beckett wrote the play as a diversion from work on his trilogy of novels, which he has always regarded as his more significant literary achievement. He chose Roger Blin to direct the first Paris production of *Godot* because he had been impressed by Blin's direction of Strindberg's *A Dream Play*. He was also influenced by the fact that the theater was nearly empty, which was precisely the reception he expected for *Godot*. Beckett knew that he was writing a play that would irritate the typical theatergoer and felt confident that Blin would not dilute those elements, including the effect of tedium, that were likely to arouse antipathy.

When *Godot* was first performed in 1953, Beckett, approaching his forty-seventh birthday, was already known as a serious avant-garde novelist, working in a genre in which James Joyce had already established the author's right to experimentation and obscurity. *Godot* marked his first venture into a territory where indifference to the expectations of one's audience was not yet a widely recognized prerogative. Beckett's violation of the tacit agreement between the playwright and his public was, for this reason, a decided provocation.

He was more distressed than pleased by the popular success of his play partly because it distracted attention from his novels and partly because he thought that the play was frequently applauded for the wrong reasons. Audiences projected on *Godot* meanings, frequently of a theological or philosophical nature, that, Beckett insisted, simply were not there. Against such interpretations, he said that the key to the play was the literal relations among its surface features, not any presumed meanings that could be deduced from them. He told Alan Schneider, the director of the first American production of the play, that *Godot* had neither meaning nor symbolism.[6] To Schneider's question, "Who or what does Godot mean," Beckett replied, "If I knew, I would have said so in the play." Schneider also noted that, while Beckett was quite willing to discuss specific details of the play, he thought that his work should speak for itself and was perfectly willing to let its supposed meanings "fall where they may."

Many critics have ignored, some with more success than others, Beckett's own warning against the search for deeper meaning in the play. Among thematic interpretations, attempts to analyze *Godot* in Christian terms have, not surprisingly, been numerous. G. S. Fraser argues that, regardless of what Beckett's own personal beliefs may be, Christianity offers a more profound and comprehensive account of the play than any other explanatory system that may be brought to bear on its interpretation.[7] Analyzing *Godot* as a "modern morality play, on permanently Christian themes," he includes among the dramatic elements that Christianity explains the act of waiting, which calls to mind the Christian attitude of waiting for God, the tree, which evokes the Garden of Eden, and Godot himself, who "stands for an anthropomorphic image of God." Hélène Baldwin similarly recommends a religious reading of the play, which she interprets as dramatizing "the soul's individual quest."[8] For Baldwin, the play's modernity consists largely in its recognition of the embattled position of religious faith in the contemporary world: "*Waiting for Godot* is concerned with the fragmentation of Christendom and with the pathos of those faithful few who 'keep their appointment' in spite of their ignorance and apathy."

Nathan Scott, himself a professor of theology, countered these interpretations of the play with the argument that there is a significant difference between the Christian's expectation of eventual union with God and the two tramps' act of waiting for Godot.[9] For the Christian, the absence of God does not render the present moment empty; it has been given meaning by Christ's incarnation. For Vladimir and Estragon, on the contrary, there is a radical discontinuity between the emptiness of the present moment and the plenitude that they expect will follow on Godot's arrival.

Perhaps the most complex interpretation of *Godot* along religious lines is that offered by Bert States in his *The Shape of Paradox.*[10] States recognizes in *Godot* the inescapable paradox of a play whose pervasive Christian symbolism coexists with ambiguity, skepticism, and, ultimately, indifference to meaning of any sort. His analysis of the potential Christian meanings of the play is balanced by his awareness that the play also conveys a strongly modern feeling of estrangement from the Christian interpretation of reality: "*Godot* is not an old Biblical myth in modern dress but a *new myth*, or story about the plight of modern man, in old dress: it is a parable for today such as might appear in a latter-day Bible aimed at accommodating modern problems of despair and alienation."

Curtis Brooks brings an added dimension to religious interpretations of the play when he points out that meaning in *Godot* is created not only by explicitly Christian allusions but also by the play's structural elements.[11] The pattern of events in *Godot* defines the play as an example of "ritual drama," enacting the primitive opposition between life and death within the natural cycle. He also observes that the sterility that afflicts both setting and characters in the play is implicitly related to the disappearance of the maternal figure in *Godot*. Curiously, in this play structured by primitive myth and ritual, the ancient figure of the mother as fertility goddess has been almost entirely excluded. This fact suggests the possibility that readers who equate religion with the figure of the patriarchal God may, like Vladimir and Estragon, be looking toward the wrong deity for solutions to the problems posed by the play.

Other readings of *Godot* have stressed ethical rather than religious approaches to the play. Lois Cuddy, for example, offers a stimulating comparison between *Godot* and the third canto of Dante's *Inferno*, which describes the punishment inflicted on the Neutrals who, indifferent to ethical distinctions, chose neither good nor evil actions.[12] Cuddy believes that Beckett's strategy in *Godot* is to portray characters who, failing to arrive at the threshold of ethical responsibility, lack the spiritual capacity to evaluate actions with reference to moral norms. Beckett differs from Dante in that he presents their degradation in psychological rather than theological terms.

David Hesla similarly emphasizes ethical considerations as a key to the play's meaning when he observes that moral activity is the one effective antidote to the prevailing feeling of meaninglessness that *Godot* conveys.[13] He cites the few acts of charity that occur in the play, such as when Vladimir and Estragon express concern for each other or for Pozzo and Lucky, as "revealing the persistence of moral consciousness in the midst of the most unpromising circumstances."

The longing for a human community in which relationships are based on ethical norms is also the central point of Dan O. Via's analysis of *Godot*.[14] Adopting the vocabulary of Jewish philosopher Martin Buber, he argues that the principal theme of the play is "the unfulfilled search for community, for I-Thou relationships in contrast to I-It relationships." He rejects interpretations that treat Vladimir and Estragon as though they are saved by their friendship. In this judgment, the two tramps fail to fulfill their aspiration to authentic community because they are not willing to be completely available to each other.

Efforts to relate the play's ethical dimension to a larger historical vision have produced provocative interpretations. Hugh Kenner says of the trilogy of novels that Beckett was writing at the same time as *Godot* that it reflects "the dehumanization of man" that resulted from the Renaissance dream of conquering nature.[15] Other readers may wish to place the origin of dehumanization somewhat earlier than the Renaissance, but it is true that Beckett's work frequently dramatizes the dehumanizing effects of a world in which techniques of control and manipulation have undergone an extraordinary development. Kenner's judgment of the trilogy has been echoed in readings of *Godot* that see the play's historical vision as based on a contrast between a modern world marked by the degradation of human relationships and a "golden age" in which men lived together in productive harmony. Darko Suvin, for example, sees in *Godot* an indictment of the spirit of individualism that, while permitting remarkable successes in man's mastery of his environment, has nevertheless led to a decline in spirituality as well as to a weakening of man's sensual relation to the world.[16] Suvin further argues that although *Godot* does not hold out any explicit hope for an improvement in the situation that it laments, it at least implicitly awakens in the spectator a longing for a world in which human relationships are based on pre-individualistic, communal models.

A similarly historical perspective is proposed by Gabor Mihalyi, for whom *Godot* testifies that dehumanization is not an eternal and hence inescapable reality but an historically conditioned experience that we have brought on ourselves and from which we can eventually be liberated.[17] For Mihalyi, *Godot* points in the direction of a liberated future by harkening "back to an earlier, more humane world where beauty, charity, friendship and love were not strangers, and in which man was still free to be human." John Fletcher shares with these critics the belief that Beckett's purpose in *Godot* is not merely the rendering of a static and permanent situation.[18] The play is intended to act as a catalyst by uncovering the forces or circumstances that have led to the present impasse and by implying the eventual possibility of escaping from the degradation that the play has dramatized. Fletcher locates the foundation of Beckett's ethical emphasis in the work of the German philosopher, Arthur Schopenhauer, particularly in the latter's idea that human misery originates in desire and that only through the abolition of desire can one hope to achieve happiness.

Other critics have stressed the collapse of traditional values as the background to *Godot*. Martin Esslin places Beckett in the company of a group of playwrights whom he designates as belonging to the "theater of the absurd."[19] Each of these writers contributes to a typically contemporary way of understanding reality: "The hallmark of this attitude is its sense that the certitudes and unshakable basic assumptions of former ages have been swept away." Esslin credits World War ll with having destroyed such substitute religions as "faith in progress, nationalism, and various totalitarian fallacies," which had until then disguised the decline of traditional religious belief. Eugene Webb similarly interprets the play as dramatizing the discovery that the ideas and values on which we base our vision of the world are fundamentally illusory.[20] Vladimir and Estragon have been deprived of comforting myths, except for their belief in Godot, to which they cling with pathetic obstinacy. The irony of the play resides in our recognizing the futility of a vigil that still has some positive meaning for them. For Gunther Anders, the pathos of the play derives not so much from the hopelessness of the situation as from the inability of the two chief characters to rise to the challenge that it presents.[21] They should, ideally, repudiate their optimistic belief in a hopeful outcome to their situation and, instead, courageously embrace a meaningless universe.

• • •

Many members of *Godot*'s first audiences responded intuitively to the revolutionary shift away from meaning and toward surface patterns that Beckett sought to achieve in his play. The most interesting recent criticism, often influenced by Beckett's direction of the play in 1975 at the Schiller Theater in Berlin, has studied the techniques through which he achieves this goal. Kenneth Tynan, who saw the original London production of *Godot,* issued a warning against thematic interpretations of the play that retains its vigor and pertinence even today: "To state that mankind is waiting for a sign that is late in coming is a platitude which none but an illiterate would interpret as making claims to profundity."[22] Tynan thought that an area of inquiry more promising than the play's message was the way in which Beckett integrated a variety of such seemingly heterogeneous theatrical traditions as vaudeville, music hall, and parable. Tynan also recognized that the play's aesthetic effect depends on something quite different from its abstract meaning when he complimented the British director, Peter Hall, for having directed the play "with a marvelous ear for its elusive rhythms." In a similar vein, Roger Blin, who directed the original Paris production of *Godot,* likened the play to a ballet, an analogy that stresses the importance of precise rhythmical movements to it successful impact.[23]

The rigorous, choreographic precision that the play requires if it is to succeed with an audience has drawn a certain amount of criticism. Pierre Macabru, for example, commenting on the 1961 production at the Théâtre de l'Odéon, complained that the play's construction is excessively methodical: "Everything is in its place. One retort calls for another retort. They are measured and weighed, placed there where they will be most efficacious. Impulse is stifled, calculation is king."[24] Deirdre Bair, in her biography of Beckett, mentions that his 1975 Schiller Theater production drew mixed reviews: "One group thought it a superbly orchestrated production, with every movement exquisitely choreographed; the other group found it a graceless performance in which all the ebb and flow of vitality and movement had been rigidly and arbitrarily stifled so that the actors moved through their lines like automatons."[25] These criticisms notwithstanding, Beckett's attachment to this approach to *Godot* is substantiated by the fact that the 1988 production that he supervised for television and videocassette follows the Schiller Theater production in most essential details.

Beckett's precise attention to the spatial form of his play and the diminished importance that he accords to its deeper meanings was also recognized by other critics, who observed that their enthusiastic responses to *Godot* were unrelated to what the play seemed to be saying. Jacques Lemarchand, for example, recognized that the appeal of the play rested with Beckett's uncanny, and not easily describable, success in giving "life and presence" to an experience, the act of waiting, that was otherwise lacking in vitality or intensity.[26] Harold Hobson believed that the human image conveyed by *Godot* was "wildly inaccurate."[27] However, in a judgment that implies that the content of the play is in some way peripheral to its effect, he contends that what really counts in *Godot* is that Beckett "has got it wrong in a tremendous way."

Others have commented on a related phenomenon: the contrast

between the apparent meanings conveyed by the text of *Godot* and the aesthetic experience produced by a performance of the play. Alan Schneider, Beckett's American director, first saw *Godot* in its French version at the Théâtre de Babylone.[28] His initial reaction to the play suggests that the effect it produces is largely autonomous from the actual words of the text. Schneider was especially qualified to make this judgment since, by his own admission, his French was severely limited, and he was able to understand very little of the dialogue. The intense impact of the play had to be accounted for largely in terms of the play's visual elements. Schneider then talks of the disappointment he experienced when he finally obtained a copy of the English translation: "Somehow, on its closely-spaced printed pages, it seemed cold and abstract, even harsh, after the remarkable ambience I had sensed at the Babylone." In a similar vein, Fletcher and Spurling argue that only in a production that is perfectly paced are we likely to enjoy "not only the wit, but also the sheer entertainment that resides in a work unjustly thought of as gloomy and boring."[29] Gabor Mihalyi has also pointed out that although the overwhelming impression gained from reading *Godot* is one of negativity, when we see the play performed we experience the defeat of this negativity: "to read the play as a whole provides an experience that is as shattering as it is sombre and cheerless. On the stage, however, the negation of negation comes over with increased impact: stage and actors give the spectator the catharsis he seeks in vain in the book."[30]

Some of the most valuable analyses of *Godot* discuss the techniques that Beckett uses to create patterns amid the apparent shambles of his play. Fletcher and Spurling observe that the struture of *Godot* owes little to the unfolding of its dramatic action; rather, it is based on "repetition, the return of leitmotifs, and on the exact balancing of variable elements."[31] Ruby Cohn has written a comprehensive analysis of the different kinds of repetition found in *Godot* as well as the various effects produced by this device.[32] Dougald McMillan and Martha Fehsenfeld have studied in great detail Beckett's shaping of formal patterns as recorded in his production notebooks for the Schiller Theater performance.[33]

Several excellent articles have related the subversion of meaning in *Godot* to shifts in the traditional function of language and physical movement in the play. Dina Scherzer has pointed out that Beckett's use of language in *Godot* anticipates some of the preoccupations that characterize the work of the French philosopher Jacques Derrida.[34] Essentially she sees Beckett's resistance to meaning as a device for liberating other potentials in language that are normally subordinated and repressed by its rational obligations. Beckett stimulates in us the recognition "that language is not an inert substance; rather, it is a material that can be shaped and transformed."

Aspasia Velissariou argues in a similar vein that Beckett releases language from the burdensome obligation of expressing anything about the nature of reality and allowing it a kind of free play.[35] Velissariou also remarks pertinently on the ethical significance of Beckett's devaluation of language in his work. Language itself is a source of alienation in the sense that it uproots us from a purely concrete, natural relationship with the world and forces on us an alienating, historically conditioned identity. Hence, the subversion of language serves the positive purpose of depriving linguistically defined identity of its prestige and of removing the barrier that frustrates our yearning for reunion with our original, natural selves.

Pierre Chabert, an actor-director who has worked on several occasions with Beckett, takes this line of interpretation to its furthest extreme. He observes that, contrary to the superficial impression that the human body is degraded in his plays, Beckett has in fact freed the body from its traditional expressive obligations: like language, the body in a Beckett play is not required to mean anything, nor is it subordinated to the exigencies of dramatic plot.[36] Chabert underlines the paradoxical quality of Beckett's theater: bodies are often disfigured and enfeebled, just as language is deprived of its power of conveying intelligible ideas, but the result of this negativity is the creation of plays that point to previously unsuspected theatrical potentialities. He concludes that Beckett explores the body as a theatrical object to an extent "unprecedented in theatrical history."

A READING

4

Introduction

Beckett undertook an intense study of the French philosopher René Descartes during his early years in Paris, filling several notebooks with quotations and comments. He also used Descartes as the central figure in his first published work, a poem on the subject of time entitled *Whoroscope.* The common feature uniting Descartes and Beckett is their profound and systematic skepticism. Descartes set out to challenge even the most self-evident ideas and to discover what, if anything, could withstand the unrestrained attack of his methodical doubt. Following in this tradition, Beckett creates fictional and theatrical works in which doubt is granted similarly unlimited force and scope.

In *Godot,* the negative process of dismantling traditional beliefs begins with the questioning of the Christian idea of a savior who possesses the power of bestowing salvation and damnation on men. Vladimir is much preoccupied at the beginning of the play with the story of Christ and the two thieves, and the longing for salvation to which this story appeals is frequently evoked. The play itself, however, implies that Godot, whether interpreted as a religious savior or, in secular terms, as a powerful and wealthy landowner, is not to be depended on for either spiritual or material benefits. At the same time that he questions the validity of Christian belief, Beckett also undermines the foundation of Western logic by blurring the distinction between truth and falsehood and by dispensing with the principle of causality. Furthermore, he deprives language of its prestige by showing that, far from being an instrument through which we master the world, it is really an efficient tool through which we become mastered and alienated by others. Finally, he subverts the role that human relationships play in giving order and meaning to life by completely dispensing with familial relations in *Godot* and by questioning our belief in the positive value of friendship.

It is well known that Descartes comes to certain positive conclusions in the course of his skeptical questioning. He affirms that his existence as a thinking subject is self-evident; how else could the act of thinking be possible? Beckett's refusal to accept even this certainty would seem to imply an even more radical form of doubt than Descartes. His negativity does not, however, leave us with feelings of desolation and abandonment. He takes everything away from us, and yet, if the play has worked on us successfully, we feel more liberated than robbed. This is because we intuitively recognize that the beliefs and foundations undermined by *Godot* exact a heavy price in terms of instinctual renunciation for the stability that they provide; they are more a burden than a foundation.

The fact that we enjoy being relieved of these inherited strutures seems confirmed by the laughter that the play provokes. In spite of the experience of dispossession that it portrays, *Godot* is a very funny play, whose humor derives in large part from the enjoyment that we take in seeing the rules of conventional rationality undermined. The dialogue of *Godot* abounds in broken linguistic rules that provoke laughter. When the play begins to acquire tragic overtones, this mood is suddenly broken by a gag. At the end of Act II, for example, Vladimir and Estragon's plans to hang themselves from the tree are interrupted by the falling of the latter's trousers. Lucky's second fall to the floor toward the end of Act I is both pathetic and hilarious. The relationship between Pozzo and Lucky is deeply disturbing, yet it is also an amusing circus act.

Introduction

Moments of laughter in *Godot* frequently coincide with implicit attacks on inherited beliefs. We laugh, for example, when Estragon does not know what a savior is, as though such innocence were both unthinkable and desirable. We sense the humorous incongruity in Act II when, hearing offstage sounds, Vladimir thinks that Godot has arrived, and then, a moment later, we see the savior appear in the form of the much-diminished Pozzo. The uncertain distinction between truth and falsehood leads to Estragon's incongruous reply, "Am I?," to Vladimir's innocent greeting, "So there you are again" (7). Humor enters the language of the play precisely at those moments when it loses its power of communicating intelligible ideas and turns into a game. Cause and effect, which are absent from the play as structuring principles, reappear in comic contexts, such as Vladimir's pseudo-explanation of the consequences of an erection: "Where it falls mandrakes grow. That's why they shriek when you pull them up" (12). The humanistic values of friendship and family are likewise challenged in *Godot*. The image of the married couple, for example, enters the play only in ways that produce laughter, as when Estragon describes pictures of the Dead Sea: "That's where we'll go, I used to say, that's where we'll go for our honeymoon" (8).

The sense of liberation that the play evokes through its comic elements is further experienced on the level of aesthetic form. Beckett's intense concern with movement and gesture, geometrical configurations, and patterns of repetition and difference bestow on *Godot* a highly strutured scenic space largely independent of the play's main action—that is, waiting for Godot. To the extent that our attention is focused on the unfolding of action in time, we are frustrated because the play refuses to satisfy our desire for logical development and completion. Once we have directed our attention away from this center of interest, however, we discover that the scenic space of *Godot* possesses those qualities of order and completeness denied to temporal elements of the play. Vladimir and Estragon's vigil produces frustrating repetition. However, the concrete elements of the play—props, movements, and gestures—create aesthetically satisfying patterns. The visual form of *Godot* should lead us to conclude that to the nihilistic Beckett (who goes much further than Descartes ever imagined possible in the subversion of inherited beliefs and traditions) should be added Beckett the artist, who has at his disposal regenerative sources denied to the rationalist philosopher.

There is, to be sure, an element of bleakness in Beckett's world: the human individual is shown bereft of those beliefs that have traditionally sustained him. However, just as Descartes' systematic doubt, which seemed to deprive him of any possible point of reference, leads him finally to discover concepts whose certainty has been assured by the fury of his skepticism, so also Beckett, after destroying every conceivable foundation, proposes alternative forms that have little connection with our conscious wishes.

Our enjoyment of *Godot*, in spite of its discouraging portrayal of human aspiration, may imply the existence of potentialities that refuse the narrow structures of conscious desire and seek expression in the fullness of the present rather than in a perpetually deferred future. Ultimately, we accept the overthrow of desire because it permits the recovery of capacities that have atrophied under its reign.

5

Christianity

Waiting for Godot presents us with the curious phenomenon of a play whose visual symbolism and central action, as well as frequent verbal exchanges, encourage Christian interpretation even though the author of the play is himself decidedly a nonbeliever. When his mother and brother were approaching death, he realized that their faith brought them no consolation: "It has no more depth than an old school tie."[37] Although admitting that he grew up in an environment saturated with the outward signs of religious faith, Beckett insists that his play should not be interpreted as implying any religious affiliation or allegiance; he simply uses Christian allusions when they serve his dramatic intentions.

Roger Blin describes the play's Christian references as the inevitable cultural baggage of any Irish writer.[38] According to Blin, even though Beckett himself is an atheist, he was born in Catholic Ireland, into a very Protestant family, a biographical fact that influences his work but only in incidental ways. He also echoes the view that when Beckett was awarded the Nobel Prize for literature, the committee mistakenly thought that it was awarding this honor to a religious writer.

Spectators who attribute religious meaning to *Godot* are not, however, entirely blameworthy. Even before the dialogue itself begins, we are likely to detect biblical overtones in details of the setting, beginning with the tree, which recalls both the forbidden tree in the Garden of Eden and the cross on which Christ was crucified. Godot's choice of this spot (Vladimir: "He said by the tree" [10]) for the anticipated meeting very likely awakens multiple associations in the Christian reader. Further, the uncertainty concerning details of their arrangement with Godot—is this the right spot? will he really come?—may remind some readers of the enigmatic behavior of the Christian God.

Along with this implicit visual prompting, the text of *Godot* contains several explicit references to the Bible, including Vladimir's half-remembered phrase from *Proverbs*—"Hope deferred maketh the something sick, who said that?" (8)—and his thwarted effort to engage Estragon in a discussion of the Gospels:

> *Vladimir:* Do you remember the Gospels?
>
> *Estragon:* I remember the maps of the Holy Land. Coloured they were. Very pretty. The Dead Sea was pale blue. The very look of it made me thirsty.(8)

His discussion of the story of the two thieves points to the possible unreliability of the documentary evidence on which the Christian faith is based:

> *Vladimir:* But all four [evangelists] were there. And only one speaks of a thief being saved. Why believe him rather than the others?
>
> *Estragon:* Who believes him?
>
> *Vladimir:* Everybody. It's the only version they know.
>
> *Estragon:* People are bloody ignorant apes. (9)

Other details of the text may also have religious implications. When Estragon is quizzing Vladimir about the agreed-on time for their meeting with Godot, he names the days of the week associated with

Christ's death and resurrection: "But what Saturday? And is it Saturday? Is it not rather Sunday? (*Pause.*) Or Monday? (*Pause.*) Or Friday?" (11). An explicit allusion to this historical event appears in Estragon's remark that where Christ lived "they crucified quick" (34). To these references may be added the possibility that the white-bearded Godot is intended to evoke the image of the Old Testament God and that Lucky is a representation of Christ as the suffering servant.

We may suspect, however, especially toward the end of the play, when Estragon admits that all his life he has been comparing himself to Christ, that Beckett is slyly suggesting that those of us who project such interpretations on details of *Godot* place ourselves in rather dubious company. Indeed, the entire play seems to be constructed as a trap intended to show us that its Christian meaning is as much the result of our own cultural inertia as it is a legitimate inference based on the objective evidence of the play. *Godot* may in part be considered a play whose pedagogical value lies not in its positive use of Christian myth as a means of interpreting the world but in its capacity for making us self-consciously critical of our own readiness to make interpretations in terms of inherited points of reference that, for the author, need not possess any inherent value.

The fundamental insight that informs all of Beckett's work consists in the recognition that our relationship to the world is based on a misunderstanding: while we assume that our individual selves are the center of the universe, the truth of the matter is that the universe, having no need of us whatsoever, acts in accordance with principles that are completely indifferent to our individual needs and aspirations. Christianity occupies an important position in *Godot* because it is one of the most potent and enduring myths through which the truth of this simple recognition has been obscured. Beckett treats the hope of salvation as an illusion, in the special sense given to that word by Sigmund Freud when he defines an illusion, in contradistinction to a mere mistake, as a false idea that contains an element of wish fulfillment. A mistake is due to a correctable intellectual failing, while an illusion is created and kept in existence, even in the face of decisive counterevidence, by the psychic need to believe that we live in a compliant world. The historical achievement of Christianity, which Beckett subjects to skeptical scrutiny, is to have encouraged the belief that the indignities of daily life, the constant reminder of how little we are actually worth, are rendered insignificant by the promise that we may eventually be saved.

The most famous allusion to the theme of salvation, which remains throughout the play as an implicit point of reference, is Vladimir's account of the story of the two thieves. The episode begins comically with Estragon's failure to understand a key term:

Vladimir: Two thieves, crucified at the same time as our Saviour. One—

Estragon: Our what?

Vladimir: Our Saviour. Two thieves. One is supposed to have been saved and the other . . . (*he searches for the contrary of saved*) . . . damned.

Estragon: Saved from what?

Vladimir: Hell.

Estragon: I'm going. (9)

Whether or not we choose to interpret Godot as a representation of God (Beckett insists, correctly but not with unimpeachable pertinence, that the pun does not work in French, the language in which the play was originally written), there can be no doubt that Vladimir and Estragon continue to wait for him because they live in a world that has been molded by the Christian hope of salvation. When they speak of having asked for a favor in the form of "A kind of prayer" or "A vague supplication" (13), we are not required to take these metaphors as establishing a decisive link between Godot and God, as proving, in effect, that Godot *is* God. All we need do is to recognize that the terms in which their request was addressed to Godot presuppose the existence of a world in which supernatural powers may be inclined to grant us the favors that we ask of them.

Although Beckett neither proves nor disproves the objective value of Christian beliefs in *Godot,* he does suggest the ease with which they lend themselves to appropriation by our egotistical needs. Even if the foundations of Christianity were to be dealt a deathblow, its vision would assume transplanted form within some secular ideology because the promise of an outcome that ultimately justifies the accumulated frustrations of a lifetime is simply too seductive an illusion to give up. Hence, throughout the play Beckett shows characters who, living in a world from which the intellectual and emotional foundations of traditional Christianity have disappeared, act as though salvation may yet be achieved in this world.

Some readers have felt that Vladimir and Estragon do achieve a form of salvation through their fidelity to Godot. According to this view, the two main characters may at least be credited with not falling quite as low as Pozzo and Lucky, whose pathetic situation may be blamed on the fact that they ignore the existence of Godot. However, Beckett himself places this affirmation in serious doubt by attributing it to Vladimir, who has done nothing to give us any confidence in the reliability of his judgment. His plea to Estragon that he join him in helping Pozzo takes the form of an inspirational burst of rhetorical puffery:

> What are we doing here, *that* is the question. And we are blessed in this, that we happen to know the answer. Yes, in this immense confusion one thing alone is clear. We are waiting for Godot to come. . . . We have kept our appointment and that's an end to that. We are not saints, but we have kept our appointment. How many people can boast as much? (51).

We are thankful to Estragon for his answer ("Billions") because it deflates Vladimir's self-important posturing. Waiting for Godot does not demonstrably make Vladimir and Estragon better then they would be in the absence of such a purposive project, but it does arguably make them much worse than they need be. Whatever sympathy they evoke in us is contravened by their irritating egotism, which is less noticed because of Pozzo's more histrionic exhibition of that frailty but is nonetheless an important motive underlying their behavior. Whether Godot is God or a wealthy landowner, they hope that he will save them, but the expectation of some form of salvation has only enfeebled them and led to their present state of paralysis. We witness the degradation that the Christian promise of salvation can encourage with special poignancy at those moments when Vladimir thinks that the moment of their deliverance may indeed be at hand: "It's Godot! At last! Gogo! It's Godot! We're saved! Let's go and meet him!" (47). The offstage sounds that have inspired Vladmir's celebratory mood merely announce the imminent appearence of Pozzo and Lucky. In Act II the arrival of the second couple, who fall in a heap at the center of the stage, inspires yet another improbable outburst:

> *Vladimir:* We are no longer alone, waiting for the night, waiting for Godot, waiting for . . . waiting. All evening we have struggled, unassisted. Now it's over. It's already to-morrow.
>
> *Pozzo:* Help!
>
> *Vladimir:* Time flows again already. The sun will set, the moon rise, and we away . . . from here. (50)

The spectacle of Vladimir thinking that he will be saved by another character whose situation is even more desperate than his own is one of the most memorable images through which Beckett comments ironically on man's hope for magical solutions to the problems of living.

Beckett's refusal to grant a privileged position to the ego and its demands appears to align him with views associated with certain oriental religions. The German philosopher Arthur Schopenhauer, whom Beckett recognized as an important intellectual influence, was convinced as to the essential truth of the oriental teaching that the waking self, the ego, was only the most superficial aspect of the human individual and a constant source of illusion. At one point he observes, with obvious relish, that Christian missionaries had not enjoyed notable success in persuading Buddhists and Hindus of the superiority of Christian doctrines. The reason for this is simple: the religions of the East are much older than Christianity, whose doctrines, including the idea of personal salvation, appear to their spiritual elders as just the sort of mistakes one would expect from a newcomer. Schopenhauer's belief in the spiritual superiority of oriental philosophers leads to the intriguing prophecy that Christianity will never succeed in India: because the primitive wisdom of the human race will not allow itself to be diverted from its natural course, it is more likely that the ancient wisdom of India will infiltrate Europe, causing the collapse of our relatively recent, and vulnerable, Christian ways of interpreting the world.

If we return to Beckett's assertion that he used Christianity when it served his dramatic intentions, we may indeed wonder if one of those intentions might not be to dramatize, like Yeats in *The Second Coming*, the return of that primitive wisdom that Christianity succeeded in repressing for a certain time but whose reappearance prefigures the end of the Christian era. In the exchange between Vladimir and Estragon with which the play begins, Vladimir is certainly right in saying to himself, "you haven't tried everything" (7), but he is condemned never to discover, except for a brief respite from his illusions, just how incomplete his inventory of human spiritual resources has been.

The one moment of authentic spiritual insight granted to Vladimir occurs toward the end of the play when he likens his self-absorption to the act of sleeping and recognizes that it has rendered him indifferent to human pain: "Was I sleeping, while the others suffered? Am I sleeping now? . . . The air is full of our cries. (*He listens.*) But habit is a great deadener"(58). Throughout the play we are reminded of the pervasiveness of suffering in the world; we also witness several episodes in which characters are invited to forget their personal misery and to respond to the needs of others. They succeed on rare occasions: Vladimir does give Estragon something to eat, and, together, they do manage to lift the fallen Lucky, and later Pozzo, to their feet. More frequently, however, they prove the validity of Vladimir's observation that "habit is a great deadener" by ignoring these cries and pursuing illusory forms of salvation.

6

Truth

All the characters in *Godot* allude in some way to the distinction between truth and falsehood. Lucky declares that the affirmations pronounced in his monologue are "established beyond all doubt" (28). Pozzo, recovering from an outburst in which he claims that Lucky is driving him mad, assures Vladimir and Estragon that there "wasn't a word of truth" (23) in this statement. Estragon makes implicit appeal to a world in which truth may be distinquished from falsehood when he accuses Godot's messenger of deceiving them: "That's all a pack of lies. (*Shaking the boy by the arm.*) Tell us the truth!" (33). Vladimir, however, concludes the first phase of his "Was I sleeping" (58) speech by suggesting that this distinction has become problematic:

> To-morrow, when I wake, or think I do, what shall I say of to-day? That with Estragon my friend, at this place, until the fall of night, I waited for Godot? That Pozzo passed, with his carrier, and that he spoke to us? Probably. But in all that what truth will there be? (58)

Vladimir's uncertainty about the meaning of what has happened during the day and his further hesitation as to whether he will actually be awake tomorrow or merely think that he is suggest that the status of truth has become extremely precarious in *Godot*.

There is scarcely a page in the text that does not remind us of the main characters' profound ignorance with regard to nearly every question that can be raised concerning their situation. They are not really sure who Godot is:

> *Pozzo:* Who is he?
> *Vladimir:* Oh he's a . . . he's a kind of acquaintance.
> *Estragon:* Nothing of the kind, we hardly know him.
> *Vladimir:* True . . . we don't know him very well . . . but all the same . . .
> *Estragon:* Personally I wouldn't even know him if I saw him. (16)

They are equally vague concerning the nature of their request to Godot and the likelihood of its being granted:

> *Estragon:* A kind of prayer.
> *Vladimir:* Precisely.
> *Estragon:* A vague supplication.
> *Vladimir:* Exactly.
> *Estragon:* And what did he reply?
> *Vladimir:* That he'd see.
> *Estragon:* That he couldn't promise anything. (13)

Their uncertainty also extends to the time and place of the expected meeting. Vladimir begins with the confident assertion that they have found the right place because Godot said "by the tree" and there is no other tree around. Estragon's remark that the tree "looks to me more like a bush" (10), however, evokes from Vladimir the worried response: "A—. What are you insinuating? That we've come to the wrong place?" (10). A moment later, Vladimir is forced to admit that he does not even know whether they have come at the right time: "He said Saturday. (*Pause.*) I think" (10).

Several pages of the text deal with the question of why Lucky does not put down his bags. This question is delayed, forgotten, taken up again, and finally answered with apparent assurance by Pozzo who seems to have been spared the uncertainties that plague Vladimir and Estragon. Even Pozzo, however, finds himself in a play in which the reign of doubting afflicts everyone. After explaining confidently that Lucky carries his bags because he wants to impress him, hoping in this way to be maintained in his degrading yet apparently desirable position as his slave, Pozzo himself falls victim to the doubting mania that has infiltrated the play:

> *Pozzo:* Ah! Why couldn't you say so before? Why he doesn't make himself comfortable? Let's try and get this clear. Has he not the right to? Certainly he has. It follows that he doesn't want to. There's reasoning for you. And why doesn't he want to? (*Pause.*) Gentlemen, the reason is this.
>
> *Vladimir:* (*to Estragon*). Make a note of this.
>
> *Pozzo:* He wants to impress me, so that I'll keep him.
>
> *Estragon:* What?
>
> *Pozzo:* Perhaps I haven't got it quite right. He wants to mollify me, so that I'll give up the idea of parting with him. No, that's not exactly it either. (21)

As spectators of the play, we experience the same difficulty as characters in arriving at certainty. When we try, for example, to understand the relationship between the two acts of the play, there seems to be no absolutely reliable way of establishing even so simple a thing as their temporal relationship. The stage directions tell us that the setting of Act II is "*Next day. Same time. Same place,*" but this affirmation contradicts certain details, such as the presence of leaves on the previously barren tree and the physical afflictions that have befallen Pozzo and Lucky, both of which would suggest a longer passage of time.

The radical uncertainty that pervades *Godot* is not limited to specific instances where the judgment of characters seems liable to error. Descartes, Beckett's great precursor in the realm of methodical doubt, had already pushed that kind of skepticism to an unsurpassable extreme. Recognizing that his senses had misled him in the past, Descartes decided that he should mistrust them entirely as a means of achieving certainty. He did conclude, however, that he could not call into question the fact that he was thinking, which implied in turn the self-evidence of his own existence. This discovery of his indubitable existence as a thinking subject led Descartes to the celebrated formulation "I think, therefore, I am."

Descartes thought that it was impossible to doubt that one was engaged in the act of thinking. Beckett, however, shows that nothing could be simpler. Vladimir and Estragon doubt not only that they have come to the right place at the right time but even that they are capable of thinking. At times they recognize that they are actively intent on avoiding thought:

> *Estragon:* In the meantime let us try and converse calmly, since we are incapable of keeping silent.
>
> *Vladimir:* You're right, we're inexhaustible.
>
> *Estragon:* It's so we won't think. (40)

This opposition between thinking and speaking, which contradicts our commonsensical assumption that they are interrelated, is reinforced a moment later when Estragon dismisses their conversations as mere blather: "Yes, now I remember, yesterday evening we spent blathering about nothing in particular. That's been going on now for half a century" (42). The most radical questioning of their ability to think occurs when, in response to Vladimir's assertion, "What is terrible is to *have* thought," Estragon replies with disarming innocence, "But did that ever happen to us?" (41). Pozzo tells Vladimir and Estragon, while casting doubt on their own mental capacities, that Lucky once possessed the unusual ability not only to think but to articulate his thoughts; unfortunately, his capacity for thinking has suffered a serious decline:

> *Pozzo:* What do you prefer? Shall we have him dance, or sing, or recite, or think, or—
>
> *Estragon:* Who?

Pozzo: Who! You know how to think, you two?

Vladimir: He thinks?

Pozzo: Certainly. Aloud. He even used to think very prettily once, I could listen to him for hours. Now . . . (*he shudders*). So much the worse for me. Well, would you like him to think something for us? (26)

The discrediting of mental operations in *Godot* seems to extend even to the word "think," which never appears in a context that confers any prestige on the act of thinking. Sometimes it introduces ideas or beliefs that are clearly false, as when Vladimir, on first seeing Estragon at the beginning of Act I, declares, "I thought you were gone for ever" (7). At other times the phrase "I think" loses its Cartesian dignity by becoming synonymous with "I guess":

Estragon: You're sure it was this evening?

Vladimir: What?

Estragon: That we were to wait.

Vladimir: He said Saturday. (*Pause.*) I think.

Estragon: You think. (10)

Wherever they appear in the play, the word "think" as well as the activity of thinking are always associated with doubt rather than with any positive or credible assertion.

As we reflect further on the radical skepticism that pervades *Godot,* we discover that Beckett has not only filled his play with examples of false judgments or with moments that call into question the solidity of the thinking subject. He has taken the further step, whose possibility eluded Descartes, of attacking the foundation on which rational thought depends: the law of contradiction. This law stipulates that a thing cannot be itself and not itself at the same time. The statement "Vladimir is heavier than Estragon" cannot coexist with the contrary affirmation "Estragon is heavier than Vladimir." Likewise, the spot where they are waiting for Godot cannot be both the right place and not the right place.

Truth

The law of contradiction is the most fundamental of all logical propositions because its violation, whereby something could simultaneously be "A" and "not A," effectively paralyzes the act of thinking. It would be impossible to distinguish truth from falsehood, the essential ambition of rational thought, if the boundary between the two were to become blurred.

Some details of *Godot*, conforming to this law, do lend themselves to logical analysis and the establishment of clear distinctions. One of the simplest illustrations occurs when Estragon asks Vladimir to give him a carrot:

> *Estragon:*   Give me a carrot. (*Vladimir rummages in his pockets, takes out a turnip and gives it to Estragon who takes a bite out of it. Angrily.*) It's a turnip!
>
> *Vladimir:*   Oh pardon! I could have sworn it was a carrot.

After rummaging once again, he succeeds in producing a carrot, a fact confirmed a moment later by Estragon:

> *Vladimir:*   How's the carrot?
>
> *Estragon:*   It's a carrot. (14)

This episode represents in simplest form the efficient operation of the law of contradiction; the vegetable that Vladimir produces either is or is not the kind that Estragon asked for. No confusion between these two alternatives is possible.

The possibility of making such clear distinctions is affirmed at several other points in the play. The story of the two thieves alludes to the opposed destinies of salvation and damnation, a point that Vladimir underlines in his remark to Estragon, "One of the thieves was saved. (*Pause.*) It's a reasonable percentage" (8). Pozzo says that the world may be divided between those who cry and those who do not: "The tears of the world are a constant quantity. For each one who begins to weep somewhere else another stops. The same is true of the laugh" (22). The same principle seems even to apply to his lungs: "My left lung is very weak! . . . But my right lung is as sound as a bell!" (27). Finally, Godot's messenger establishes a clear distinction between himself, who minds the goats, and his brother, who minds the sheep (33).

At the same time, however, Beckett introduces details that subvert these distinctions. An obvious example occurs with the arrival in Act II of the "second" messenger. We "know" that this is the same boy who appeared at the end of the first act, yet he claims otherwise:

> Boy: Mister . . . (*Vladimir turns.*) Mister Albert . . .
> Vladimir: Off we go again. (*Pause.*) Do you not recognize me?
> Boy: No Sir.
> Vladimir: It wasn't you came yesterday.
> Boy: No Sir.
> Vladimir: This is your first time.
> Boy: Yes Sir. (58)

The boy who was so clearly distinguished from his brother at the end of Act I seems now to have become merged with him. What is at stake in this exchange is not simply the difficulty of deciding whether the boy is telling the truth or not but, rather, the way in which his insistence that he *is not* the messenger whom we know he *is* draws us into a world that lies beyond the barrier erected by the law of contradiction and that cannot be judged by its criteria. This law is further subverted in the second act when Vladimir appears to have found Estragon's shoes (43). We know that they are the same shoes that Estragon left on stage at the end of the first act, but his repeated insistence that they are a different pair of boots attacks our rational certainties at their foundation. A parallel challenge to the law of contradiction occurs when Vladimir dissipates the distinction between the two thieves by recalling that one of the evangelists says that *both* of them abused Christ (9). Likewise, the difference between laughing and crying is implicitly questioned by a play that Beckett subtitled a "tragicomedy" and that illustrates the paradoxical affirmation made in *Endgame* that "nothing is funnier than unhappiness."

Truth

Beckett's undermining of the law of contradiction does not mean, however, that truth is entirely banished from the play. On the contrary, the disappearance of rational, noncontradictory forms of truth prepares the way for the apparition of kinds of truths that are obscured by the reign of purely rational criteria. Beckett reminds us at several points in the play that the life of feeling cannot be reduced to neat oppositions; it is frequently marked by ambivalence, the copresence of antithetical emotions.

Vladimir illustrates this refusal of our emotions to submit to logic when he muses on "the last moment"—that is, the eventuality of his own death: "Sometimes I feel it coming all the same. Then I go all queer.... How shall I say? Relieved and at the same time ... (*he searches for the word*) ... appalled. (*With emphasis.*) AP—PALLED" (8). Similarly, we are reminded throughout the play of the contradictory nature of the relationship between Vladimir and Estragon. They are forever complaining that they would be better off alone, and yet they continually return to each other. Again, it is Vladimir who best expresses their ambivalence: "I missed you ... and at the same time I was happy. Isn't that a queer thing? (38). A comparable ambiguity surrounds the relationship between Pozzo and Lucky. At first glance, we assume that Pozzo is the master and Lucky the slave. Beckett diminishes the initial clarity of this schema, however, by having Pozzo complain that real power is in the hands of Lucky: "He used to be so kind ... so helpful ... and entertaining ... my good angel ... and now ... he's killing me" (23). Our commonsensical assumption that one must be either master or slave, and not both at the same time, receives striking disconfirmation in this speech.

The suspension of the law of contradiction in *Godot* permits Beckett to dramatize the truth of unconscious experience, which ignores the existence of such law. Although the rational activities that we undertake in waking life depend on the maintenance of the distinction between "A" and "not A," dreaming, and the unconscious processes that it reveals, is entirely liberated from such constraints. Hence, mobility and stasis are logically distinct categories in waking life, but they may coexist in dreams and in *Godot:*

39

Estragon: Well, shall we go?
Vladimir: Yes, let's go.
           They do not move. (35)

Likewise, those details of the play—such as Estragon's boots that are not his boots and the second messenger who is not himself but his brother—that defy normal criteria for establishing truth are, for this very reason, a truthful means of representing what happens when we dream.

Vladimir and Estragon's actions frequently exhibit this irrational quality of dreams. Just after chastising Pozzo for throwing Lucky away "like a banana skin," for example, they do an abrupt about-face and accuse Lucky of "crucifying" his master (22–23). The fact that an enjoyable dream can, without any apparent provocation, turn into a nightmare is mirrored by their behavior when they think that Godot is about to appear. Vladimir greets his impending arrival with a speech that expresses his sense of liberation: "It's Godot! At last! Gogo! It's Godot! We're saved! Let's go and meet him!" (47). The next instant, however, his joy is transformed into the implausible, nightmarish fear that they will not be able to escape from their redeemer: "We're surrounded! (*Estragon makes a rush towards back.*) Imbecile! There's no way out there" (47).

A very different kind of truth that survives the disintegrative tendencies of *Godot* is the truth of suffering. We cannot know who Godot is or why he keeps Vladimir and Estragon waiting. The existence of suffering, however, is incontrovertible. Even before the first line of dialogue is spoken, the stage directions describe Estragon as "panting" and "exhausted" from the effort of trying to remove his boots. We learn from his first conversation with Vladimir that he spent the preceding night in a ditch, where he was beaten. A moment later, we learn that both Vladimir and Estragon suffer from constant physical pain:

Estragon: (*feebly*). Help me!
Vladimir: It hurts?
Estragon: (*angrily*). Hurts! He wants to know if it hurts!

Truth

Vladimir: (*angrily*). No one ever suffers but you. I don't count. I'd like to hear what you'd say if you had what I have.

Estragon: It hurts?

Vladimir: (*angrily*). Hurts! He wants to know if it hurts! (7)

Lucky, who spends the greater part of Act I standing at center stage, weighed down by the burden of the baggage he is carrying, also suffers the further indignity of a running sore, caused by the rope attached to his neck and examined at some length by Vladimir and Estragon (17). Even Pozzo, who boasts that he is incapable of suffering, has anxieties about the condition of his heart and lungs. He is also painfully aware of the precariousness of life: "They give birth astride of a grave, the light gleams an instant, then it's night once more" (57). The constancy of suffering is an absolutely reliable point of reference throughout *Godot*. Every other certainty may disintegrate under the pressure of Beckett's radical skepticism, but if suffering undergoes any change in the play, it is in the direction of a worsening that only confirms its indestructibility.

This unalterable truth of suffering is the subject of Lucky's great monologue, which, despite its superficial incoherence, conveys a lucid and, on the evidence of the play, entirely valid proposition: in spite of all of his efforts to prevent his decline, man "wastes and pines wastes and pines" (29). While Vladimir and Estragon hope for some alleviation of their predicament, Lucky recognizes that man's fate is to experience a deepening of his suffering and eventually to die:

> alas alas on on the skull the skull the skull the skull in Connemara
> in spite of the tennis the labors abandoned left unfinished graver
> still abode of stones in a word I resume alas alas abandoned unfin-
> ished the skull the skull in Connemara in spite of the tennis the
> skull alas the stones Cunard (*mêlée, final vociferations*) tennis . . .
> the stones . . . so calm . . . Cunard . . . unfinished . . . (29)

Descartes' search for fundamental truth led him to affirm the indestructible existence of the thinking subject; to this, Lucky opposes the image of the skull, with the shift from cerebration to mortality that it portends. *Godot* itself would seem to encourage the conclusion that Descartes' appeal to the rational act of thinking as proof of his existence is no longer convincing. Since the primacy that Descartes ascribed to thought seems more an attribute of suffering, his dictum might be rewritten: "I suffer, therefore, I am."

7

Language

Several readers of *Godot* called attention to a striking feature of the language of the play: although words spoken by characters often fail to communicate thoughts, they do supply the raw material for a series of verbal games that we instinctively enjoy even though they may be largely lacking in intelligible content. Moreover, when language does fulfill its communicative function in *Godot*, it frequently serves as an instrument of oppression and alienation. The intelligibility of a statement is often directly proportional to its success in manipulating a character's behavior. The playful use of words, on the contrary, deprives language of its coercive power, transforming it into an expression not of authority but of liberated impulses.

The contrast between the dramatization of language's authority and its subversion is well illustrated by two examples of dialogue between Vladimir and Estragon. In the most frequently repeated exchange in the play, Vladimir prevents Estragon from leaving the stage by reminding him that they must wait for Godot:

Estragon: Let's go.
Vladimir: We can't.

Estragon: Why not?
Vladimir: We're waiting for Godot.
Estragon: (*despairingly*). Ah! (31–32)

Here, the efficacy of language is beyond dispute. Estragon has not the slighest difficulty in understanding what Vladimir means, and he submits his bodily movements to the command implicit in his partner's reminder. At the other extreme, we have the famous exchange with which each act of the play ends:

Estragon: Well, shall we go?
Vladimir: Yes, let's go.
　　　　　They do not move.

In this case, the connection between language and action is abrogated. Physical gesture, which in the first example is entirely subordinated to words, now achieves autonomy.

The difference between these two episodes in *Godot* serves as a model for an opposition that pervades the play. On the other hand, we find dramatic representations of oppression that call attention especially to the ways in which language, the supposed instrument of rationality and liberation, is used to mystify and to oppress. On the other hand, the play abounds in devices—including ambiguity, wordplay, and the use of physical gestures—that deprive language of its coercive power.

Perhaps the most memorable example of the equation that *Godot* establishes between intelligibility and oppression appears in those scenes where Pozzo is shouting commands at Lucky. Unlike Estragon and Vladimir, whose conversations are frequently marked by ambiguity and misconstruals, Lucky knows perfectly well what Pozzo wants. Each of his gestures is a correct response to his master's verbal commands:

Up hog! (*Noise of Lucky getting up and picking up his baggage. Pozzo jerks the rope.*) Back! (*Enter Lucky backwards.*) Stop! (*Lucky stops.*) Turn! (*Lucky turns. To Vladimir and Estragon, affably.*)

Language

Gentlemen, I am happy to have met you. (*Before their incredulous expression.*) Yes yes, sincerely happy. (*He jerks the rope.*) Closer! (*Lucky advances.*) Stop! (*Lucky stops.*) (16).

The commands that Pozzo addresses to Lucky represent an implicit condemnation of language's usefulness in arranging the degradation of one human being by another. Beckett also conveys this critique of language in an especially forceful and memorable way through the metaphoric link that he establishes between Pozzo's rope and whip and his words. Shouting a verbal command at an underling is equivalent to tugging on the rope that is tied around his neck or urging him on through the crack of a whip.

The authority that Godot exerts over Vladimir and Estagon is a less obvious but equally constraining creation of language. Vladimir would not be insisting that they return to the same spot each evening if it were not for a verbal promise made by Godot. Furthermore, he relies on language to persuade Estragon of the reasonableness of their vigil. In however vague terms, he conveys the idea that life will be better when Godot arrives. He also uses words to guarantee that Estragon will not obey his spontaneous desire to give up waiting. Not only does he repeat the ritual reminder that they are obliged to wait, but he also warns of some unspecified harm that will befall them if they do not:

Vladimir:	We have to come back to-morrow.
Estragon:	What for?
Vladimir:	To wait for Godot.
Estragon:	Ah! (*Silence.*) He didn't come?
Vladimir:	No.
Estragon:	And now it's too late.
Vladimir:	Yes, now it's night.
Estragon:	And if we dropped him? (*Pause.*) If we dropped him?
Vladimir:	He'd punish us. (59)

Another illustration of the way that language allows us to fall victim to alienating representations of reality occurs when Vladimir recounts the story of Christ and the two thieves. This story, along with the related allusions to Christianity, underlines the repressive effects of myths, which could not exist in the absence of language. The story does not so much explain anything about reality as it imprisons Vladimir within a crippling hierarchy, in which a figure whose authority is beyond question may choose either to save or damn him. His constant preoccupation with this subject, his expectation that they will be saved by Godot's arrival, and his fear that they are damned without him, dramatize the degradation of an individual whose mind has become paralyzed by words and the obscurantist myths that they impose.

Language is further indicted as a source of repression when Vladimir uses it to advise Estragon that they no longer have any rights:

> *Vladimir:* Your Worship wishes to assert his prerogatives?
>
> *Estragon:* We've no rights any more?
>
> *Laugh of Vladimir, stifled as before, less the smile.*
>
> *Vladimir:* You'd make me laugh if it wasn't prohibited.
>
> *Estragon:* We've lost our rights?
>
> *Vladimir:* (*distinctly*). We got rid of them.
>
> *Silence. They remain motionless, arms dangling, heads sunk, sagging at the knees.* (13)

Vladimir's distinctly conveyed warning resembles many other clear, unequivocal statements in *Godot* whose success in communicating intelligible ideas results in a loss of personal autonomy.

Beckett deploys a variety of strategies designed to thwart this alienating power of language and its capacity for inflicting crippling ideas on us. One of the simplest devices, which attacks the authoritarian potential of language at its heart, consists in foregrounding the ambiguity of words. *Godot* begins with an example of this strategy. Estragon has been wrestling unsuccessfully with his boots. At last, he gives up, exclaiming: "Nothing to be done" (7). Vladimir, who does not know the reason for his partner's exclamation, responds in a completely inappropriate way: "I'm beginning to come round to that opinion. All my life I've tried to put it from me, saying, Vladimir, be reasonable, you haven't tried everything. And I resumed the struggle" (7). Estragon's distress is limited to the problem of removing his boots; Vladimir is concerned with difficulties of a more metaphysical sort that prevent his recognizing the prosaic source of his partner's complaint. We could interpret this initial exchange negatively, as illustrating a breakdown of communication, but we should realize at the same time that, given the coercive nature of successful communication in the play, this breakdown is not entirely undesirable.

A related device for diminishing the communicative power of language consists in having characters speak in non sequiturs. For example, Estragon's effort to enlist Vladimir's aid in removing his boot, leads to the following exchange:

Vladimir: (*gloomily*). It's too much for one man. (*Pause. Cheerfully.*) On the other hand what's the good of losing heart now, that's what I say. We should have thought of it a million years ago, in the nineties.

Estragon: Ah stop blathering and help me off with this bloody thing.

Vladimir: Hand in hand from the top of the Eiffel Tower, among the first. We were respectable in those days. Now it's too late. They wouldn't even let us up. (*Estragon tears at his boot.*) What are you doing? (7)

Even when Vladimir finally does direct his attention to Estragon's problem, his response is not to help him but to deliver an irrelevant lecture: "Boots must be taken off every day, I'm tired telling you that. Why don't you listen to me?" (7). A moment later Estragon proves himself equally capable of the disarming irrelevancy:

Vladimir: Do you remember the Gospels?

Estragon: I remember the maps of the Holy Land. Coloured they were. Very pretty. (8)

The failure of communication also enters the play at moments when characters lose that distinctness of speech with which Pozzo had shouted orders at Lucky. The first interruption of this sort occurs when Estragon tries to talk while eating his carrot:

Vladimir: Well?

Estragon: (*his mouth full, vacuously*). We're not tied?

Vladimir: I don't hear a word you're saying.

Estragon: (*chews, swallows*). I'm asking you if we're tied. (14)

Later, Beckett will combine a non sequitur with the garbled pronunciation of a phrase to cause yet another temporary halt in conversation:

Vladimir: You want to get rid of him?

Pozzo: Remark that I might just as well have been in his shoes and he in mine. If chance had not willed otherwise. To each one his due.

Vladimir: You waagerrim?

Pozzo: I beg you pardon?

Vladimir: You want to get rid of him?

Pozzo: I do. (21)

Pozzo introduces a variation on this device when, in the course of recounting his past life with Lucky, he uses a word whose meaning escapes characters and audience alike:

Pozzo: Beauty, grace, truth of the first water, I knew they were all beyond me. So I took a knook.

Vladimir: (*startled from his inspection of the sky*). A knook?

Pozzo: That was nearly sixty years ago. (22)

At one point, Estragon unexpectedly slips into French, the language he speaks in the original text of the play:

Estragon: Que voulez-vous?

Vladimir: I beg your pardon?

Language

Estragon: Que voulez-vous?
Vladimir: Ah! que voulez-vous. Exactly. (42)

The creation of such gaps as these, which interrupt the normal flow of conversation and diminish its communicative efficacy, is among the principal means through which Beckett dramatizes the possibility of resisting language's authority.

The coercive power of words in *Godot* is further diluted through the creation of a concrete, physical language of movement and gesture that communicates ideas and feelings even more vividly than the verbal language of the play. The stage direction describing the posture of Vladimir and Estragon after Vladimir's comment about losing their rights is concrete and eloquent: "*They remain motionless, arms dangling, heads sunk, sagging at the knees*" (13). Words could add little to the intense impression of despair and paralysis that the tramps convey through the medium of their bodies. So also, at the beginning of the play, Estragon's mime with his recalcitrant boots conveys the hopelessness of his predicament even before he utters the first line of spoken dialogue, "Nothing to be done." Nonverbal means of communication are so highly developed in the play that members of the audience can grasp its central features even if they do not speak the language in which it is performed. The difficulty that characters have in moving about the stage, their frequent immobility and silence, and the truncated quality of so many of their gestures communicate immediately through a vivid stage image. Likewise, Pozzo's exercise of control over Lucky through rope and whip, Estragon's repeated act of falling asleep on his stone, and Vladimir's gesture of looking about the stage anxiously and expectantly achieve their effects without having to pass through the indirections of verbal language. Need, hunger, frustration, fear, and exuberance are experiences that precede the acquisition of words and that we all originally expressed with the perfectly satisfactory, and in fact unsurpassable, means of our bodies. In *Godot* Beckett restores this primitive expressiveness of the body, lost or at least greatly diminished by the learning of a language.

Finally, the prestige of language's communicative power is undermined by verbal games that add no new information but release the spontaneous playful impulses that meaningful language seeks to repress. Vladimir introduces this device at the beginning of the play when, on first seeing Estragon, he succeeds in saying the same thing in three different ways:

> *Vladimir:* So there you are again.
> *Estragon:* Am I?
> *Vladimir* I'm glad to see you back. I thought you were gone for ever.
> *Estragon:* Me too.
> *Vladimir:* Together again at last! (7)

Shortly after, Estragon will show that he can play this game as competently as Vladimir:

> *Vladimir:* Nothing you can do about it.
> *Estragon:* No use struggling.
> *Vladimir:* One is what one is.
> *Estragon:* No use wriggling.
> *Vladimir:* The essential doesn't change.
> *Estragon:* Nothing to be done. (14)

Another favored means for interrupting the forward movement of conversation and creating the effect of marching in place is the deployment of synonyms. Vladimir and Estragon's thoughts about taking exercise, for example, do not lead to any positive physical action but produce an amusing list of equivalent expressions:

> *Vladimir:* We could do our exercises.
> *Estragon:* Our movements.
> *Vladimir:* Our elevations.
> *Estragon:* Our relaxations.
> *Vladimir:* Our elongations.
> *Estragon:* Our relaxations.

Language

Vladimir: To warm us up.

Estragon: To calm us down. (49)

Similarity of meaning may also be reinforced by similarity of sound, as when their effort to curse each other produces the following series: "Moron! . . . Vermin! . . . Abortion! . . . Morpion! . . . Sewer-rat! . . . Curate . . . Cretin! . . . Crritic!" (48).

The most sophisticated use of these devices appears in Lucky's monologue (28–29). Although he experiences great difficulty in imposing grammatical connections among the words of his discourse and making it mean something, Lucky nonetheless possesses a quite formidable capacity for playing with words and, in this way, causing pleasure even when we do not understand him.

The illogical effect of the speech—the sense of a vast disproportion between what is being said and the number of words required to convey these ideas—stems from Lucky's reluctance to grant his monologue any forward movement: his constant strategy consists in interrupting its momentum so as to ensure that it will never achieve the neatness and clarity of a complete statement. Appropriately, his final word is "unfinished."

This constant interruption of the speech's momentum appears from the very beginning, where Lucky twice intrudes the meaningless and irrelevant phrase "quaquaquaqua" and includes the relevant but not quite necessary observation that the God who is the subject of the first part of his discourse is "outside time without extension." The repetition of phrases having phonetic resemblances, noted already in some of Vladimir and Estragon's games, appears in his allusion to this God's "divine apathia divine athambia divine aphasia." The pleasure of repetition of sound and image, more than the requirements of intelligible communication, similarly guides the description of the sufferings of hell: "plunged in torment plunged in fire whose fire flames if that continues and who can doubt it will fire the firmament." Throughout the speech his repetition of key phrases permits him to return to the beginning of his statement and hence avoid the obligation of leading it to a successful completion. The most important of these series is the

51

following, which recurs during the first part of the speech: "as uttered forth in the public works of Puncher and Wattmann . . . as a result of the labors left unfinished . . . as a result of the labors unfinished of Testew and Cunard . . . as a result of the public works of Puncher and Wattmann . . . in view of the labors of Fartov and Belcher" (28). Having deprived his introduction of any forward movement, Lucky will then conclude his speech in such a way that the end duplicates the beginning: "in the light of the labors lost of Steinweg and Peterman . . . in the light the light the light of the labors lost of Steinweg and Peterman . . . the labors abandoned left unfinished" (29). Likewise, when he arrives at the point in his speech in which he wants to say that all of our efforts to hide from the fact of mortality are in vain, rather than providing a simple sequence of grammatically connected words that express this idea clearly, he gives himself over to a berserk listing of the kinds of diversion by which we may be tempted: "in spite of the strides of physical culture the practice of sports such as tennis football running cycling swimming flying floating riding gliding contating camogie skating tennis of all kinds dying flying sports of all sorts autumn summer winter winter tennis of all kinds hockey of all sorts penicilline and succedanea in a word I resume flying gliding golf over nine and eighteen holes tennis of all sorts."

By employing playfulness to erode meaning, Lucky subverts those authoritarian uses of language whose aim is manipulation. The speech's comic liberation from the rules governing conventional speech prevents it from acquiring any coercive force. It utterly fails in its immediate goal of providing an entertainment for the other characters and perhaps of influencing Pozzo to keep him. However, in light of language's distressing success in manipulating behavior elsewhere in the play, Lucky's failure may legitimately be judged a stirring triumph.

8

Causality

The ability to conceive of events in the external world in terms of relations between cause and effect is a relatively late acquisition, but it is nonetheless a constant point of reference in all of our adult evaluations of the world. We have difficulty grasping that this ingrained habit of thought is merely a mental construct that, while extending our control over the world obscures deeper layers of reality. In his essay on Proust, Beckett condemns causality as a construct to which authors are obligated to submit. Because of the shortcomings of literary conventions, he tell us, a writer "is not altogether at liberty to detach effect from cause."[39]

Although not entirely liberating *Godot* from this requirement, Beckett does succeed in depriving causality of the prestige that it enjoys in traditional theater. Most playwrights assume, following principles first articulated by Aristotle in his *Poetics,* that their chief obligation is to create plots. They cannot simply furnish their plays with episodes; rather, they must accept the additional responsibility of creating logical arrangements of events with a coherent beginning, middle, and end and governed by the principle of causality. The concluding episode of a tragedy, for example, in which the hero comes to some significant discovery, must be shown to have been caused by earlier events in the play.

Godot, however, repudiates traditional practice. The main action of the play centers on an effect, the expected arrival of Godot, which is never produced. Vladimir and Estragon attempt to ensure Godot's appearance by coming to the proper place at the proper time and awaiting the logical outcome of these actions. However, Beckett treats causality ironically by, first, casting pervasive doubt on the validity and likely efficacy of the cause. Vladimir must admit, under pressure of Estragon's questioning, that the evidence for this being the agreed-on place is rather flimsy; likewise, he cannot really be sure that they have come on the right day. Beckett then deepens the irony by permitting Vladimir and Estragon's preparations to produce only substitutive effects. Pozzo and Lucky arrive in place of Godot; later, Godot's messenger appears to announce the deferral of his master's promise.

Refusing the Aristotelian requirement of a coherent beginning, middle, and end, Beckett offers a truncated version of this classical model: a beginning, in which Vladimir and Estragon arrive to await Godot, a middle, in which Godot fails to appear, but no end in which some new action results from the conflict raised in the middle of the play. A related way of understanding Beckett's break with traditional practice appears when the play is divided into its three sequential actions: Vladimir and Estragon before the arrival of Pozzo and Lucky, the arrival of the second couple, and Vladimir and Estragon after the couple's departure. The most striking feature of this three-part division is that individual phases are not related causally. If this were a traditional play, the arrival of Pozzo and Lucky, while not having the magnitude of Godot's prospective appearance, would at least exert some influence on the way in which the action of the play unfolds. But nothing of the sort happens. Vladimir and Estragon do not overpower Pozzo and force him to release Lucky; rather, ironically, when they eventually do act, it is to pummel Lucky until he falls to the floor, thus ending his "unfinished" tirade. Nor does the appearance of Lucky and Pozzo alter the course of Vladimir and Estragon's lives. They continue waiting for Godot as they would have even if Lucky and Pozzo had never appeared. In other words, Beckett does not make the initial action of the play more complex by placing it in conflict with some opposing or constraining force. Vladimir and Estragon's intention of waiting for Godot's arrival is not challenged by Pozzo's ridicule or by his making them an offer that might tempt them to renounce their vigil. Clearly Beckett does not care about traditional modes of development in which the initial action of the play is placed in confict with another, creating a certain suspense regarding the effect that their interaction will produce. The only effect achieved by the arrival of the second couple is that time passes more quickly.

Beckett's rejection of causality as a structuring principle affects all aspects of *Godot*. The opening scene of the play immediately situates us in a world where human effort is highly ineffectual. We first see Estragon experiencing improbable difficulty in removing one of his shoes. What, in a normal play, would be a trivial and easily accomplished gesture, acquires in *Godot* the significance of a major task, requiring the concentrated efforts of both Estragon and his partner and occupying a substantial period of time.

In his director's notebook for the Schiller Theater production of *Godot*, Beckett makes clear that the second most important nonaction of the play, after Godot's failure to appear, is the lack of response to appeals for help. Toward the beginning of the play Estragon pleads with Vladimir, "Help me!," to which the latter responds, rather unhelpfully, "It hurts?" (7). He repeats his request on the following page ("Why don't you help me?") but to little effect. Similar appeals for help occur repeatedly throughout the play. The longest of them begins with the return of Lucky and Pozzo in Act II. Immediately on arriving, they both fall to the ground and "*lie helpless among the scattered baggage.*" Pozzo's cries for help, in conformity to the underlying logic of the play, produce only a series of non sequiturs:

> *Pozzo:* Help!
>
> *Estragon:* Is it Godot?
>
> *Vladimir:* We were beginning to weaken. Now we're sure to see the evening out.

Pozzo:	Help!
Estragon:	Do you hear him?
Vladimir:	We are no longer alone, waiting for the night, waiting for Godot, waiting for . . . waiting. All evening we have struggled, unassisted. Now it's over. It's already to-morrow.
Pozzo:	Help!
Vladimir:	Time flows again already. The sun will set, the moon rise, and we away . . . from here. (49–50)

Pozzo's repeated cries elicit some comically bombastic speeches from Vladimir, such as his urging to Estragon, "Let us represent worthily for once the foul brood to which a cruel fate consigned us!" (51), but little effective help. When Vladimir finally does try responding to Pozzo's appeal, he succeeds only in making matters worse: "We're coming! (*He tries to pull Pozzo to his feet, fails, tries again, stumbles, falls, tries to get up, fails.*)" (52).

Yet another breakdown in the tramps' ability to produce desired effects occurs when they experience difficulties in maintaining a conversation. Their efforts to pass the time by talking usually peter out soon after they begin, obliging them, with generally unimpressive results, to find a fresh beginning:

	Silence.
Estragon:	That wasn't such a bad little canter.
Vladimir:	Yes, but now we'll have to find something else.
Estragon:	Let me see.
	He takes off his hat, concentrates.
Vladimir:	Let me see. (*He takes off his hat, concentrates. Long silence.*) Ah!
	They put on their hats, relax.
Estragon:	Well?
Vladimir:	What I was saying, we could go on from there. (42)

Their difficulty in finding ways of occupying time is especially noticeable in the second act. Lucky and Pozzo served the useful purpose, as

Causality

Vladimir observes toward the end of Act I, of causing time to pass more quickly. Their second appearance, however, is much briefer than the first, forcing Vladimir and Estragon to rely more on their own doubtful initiatives. Not surprisingly, the dialogue that they produce frequently comments on its own failure:

> *Vladimir:* Say something!
> *Estragon:* I'm trying.
> *Long silence.*
> *Vladimir:* (*in anguish*). Say anything at all!
> *Estragon:* What do we do now?
> *Vladimir:* Wait for Godot.
> *Estragon:* Ah!
> *Silence.* (40–41)

They are reduced to searching for artificial ploys that will stimulate their flagging powers: "That's the idea, let's contradict each other . . . That's the idea, let's ask each other questions" (41), "That's the idea, let's abuse each other" (48). Not only are Vladimir and Estragon incapable of causing Godot to arrive; they even fail to produce conversations that are interesting enough to allow them, or members of the audience, to forget that lamentable misfortune.

Their failure to stimulate dialogue is ironically contrasted with those moments where Vladimir succeeds in repressing Estragon's spontaneous impulse to talk:

> *Estragon:* I had a dream.
> *Vladimir:* Don't tell me.
> *Estragon:* I dreamt that—
> *Vladimir:* DON'T TELL ME! (11)

A moment later, Vladimir will impose a similar inhibition on Estragon's recital of the anecdote about the Englishman in the brothel:

Estragon: An Englishman having drunk a little more than usual proceeds to a brothel. The bawd asks him is he wants a fair one, a dark one or a red-haired one. Go on.

Vladimir: STOP IT! (11)

Frustration of the normal passage from cause to effect is not the only means by which Beckett diminishes the authority of this organizing principle. He also subjects it to comic deflation, as when he has Vladimir give Estragon a rather improbable account of the likely effects that would be produced should they decide to commit suicide:

Estragon: What about hanging ourselves?

Vladimir: Hmm. It'd give us an erection.

Estragon: (*highly excited*). An erection!

Vladimir: With all that follows. Where it falls mandrakes grow. That's why they shriek when you pull them up. (12)

Another implausible allusion to causality occurs when Pozzo tells Vladimir and Estragon that Lucky must be wearing his hat in order to think:

Vladimir: (*to Pozzo*). Tell him to think.

Pozzo: Give him his hat.

Vladimir: His hat?

Pozzo: He can't think without his hat. (27)

When, after some initial hesitation, Vladimir does place the hat on Lucky's head, the act of thinking that Pozzo has promised is, rather improbably, produced. Likewise, when Vladimir and Estragon decide to silence Lucky, the hat produces the desired effect:

Pozzo: His hat!

Vladimir seizes Lucky's hat. Silence of Lucky. He falls. Silence. Panting of the victors.

Causality

Estragon:	Avenged!
	Vladimir examines the hat, peers inside it.
Pozzo:	Give me that! (*He snatches the hat from Vladimir, throws it on the ground, tramples on it.*) There's an end to his thinking! (29–30)

This is one of the few moments in the play illustrating the successful operation of cause and effect, and it is a decidely implausible one. Another example of mock-causality appears when Pozzo explains to Estragon, who begins crying after Lucky kicks him, why the tears of the latter have suddenly stopped: "You have replaced him as it were. (*Lyrically.*) The tears of the world are a constant quantity. For each one who begins to weep somewhere else another stops. The same is true of the laugh" (22). Something resembling causality, without quite being the thing itself, also appears at the end of each act of the play when the departure of Godot's messenger seems to cause the moon to rise.

Another method used by Beckett to place in question the traditional prestige of causality is to contrast the comic inability of Vladimir and Estragon to maintain the smooth functioning of the machinery of cause and effect with the brutal and efficient power that Pozzo exercises over Lucky. Each of his shouted orders immediately produces its intended result. The slightest departure from compliance with any of his wishes is immediately corrected by another order that makes Lucky aware of his mistake. In effect, Beckett demotes causality by identifying it in our minds with the most vicious and egotistical of his characters. The characters with whom we sympathize, and from whom we may hope for some positive action, are incapable of exerting any real influence over events in the play. We recall, for example, the protest that Vladimir and Estragon undertake on behalf of Lucky. They begin by expressing vehement indignation at the inhuman treatment accorded him by Pozzo:

Vladimir:	(*exploding*). It's a scandal!
	Silence. Flabbergasted, Estragon stops gnawing, looks at Pozzo and Vladimir in turn. Pozzo outwardly calm. Vladimir embarrassed.

Pozzo:	(*to Vladimir*). Are you alluding to anything in particular?
Vladimir:	(*stutteringly resolute*). To treat a man . . . (*gesture towards Lucky*) . . . like that . . . I think that . . . no . . . a human being . . . no . . . it's a scandal!
Estragon:	(*not to be outdone*). A disgrace! (18–19)

Their abhorrence of Pozzo's behavior toward Lucky gets off to an unusually energetic start. This moral fervor subsides quickly enough, however, and the only result of their solicitude is that Lucky deals Estragon a very painful kick to the shin when the latter attempts to wipe the tears from his eyes.

It may be an additional irony of the play that relationships of cause and effect, which have little influence over the unfolding of events in the play, do achieve some prominence in the realm of physical movement. We understand that Vladimir and Estragon's limps are caused by physical ailments: one suffers from sore feet, the other has a constant pain in his groin. Similarly, we know that Vladimir's offstage flights are necessitated by pressure on his bladder. More broadly, stage movement reminds us numerous times that in a play in which rational principles, including the law of contradiction, seem to have been suspended, the law of gravity does nevertheless continue to produce predictable and intelligible effects. When Pozzo and Lucky first enter, Pozzo pulls the rope that is tied to Lucky's neck taut, causing him to fall to the ground. Throughout the middle part of the first act, Lucky stands center stage, weighed down by the burden of his baggage, which gives tangible evidence of the continued operation of gravity. Furthermore, every other major character falls at least once in the play, and a significant part of Act II is played with all four of them lying on the ground. In Act I, when they are contemplating suicide by hanging, Estragon explains the consequences of this law to Vladimir: "Gogo light—bough not break—Gogo dead. Didi heavy—bough break—Didi alone" (12). These examples may lead us to conclude that logical coherence, which Aristotle had attributed to the central action of a play, has been deprived of this eminent role and consigned to merely trivializing contexts.

Causality

Beckett dethrones causality in *Godot* because, as he indicates in his essay on Proust, it is an irritating convention having no special claim on a writer's respect. Literary works that show one event leading logically to the next successfully conform to an honored tradition but ignore the pervasiveness of irrationality and immobility, experiences that are fundamental to Beckett's artistic vision. Dispensing with causality as the organizing principle of his play further allows Beckett to foreground other kinds of patterns, such as repetition and difference, which are rooted in primitive stages of perception. We grasp resemblances and distinctions among things before we understand that one thing causes another to happen. Hence, by promoting repetition and difference over causality, Beckett restores perceptual forms that had themselves been dislodged by the arrival of cause and effect.

9

Memory and Expectation

References to past and future abound in *Godot*. Beckett frequently shows his characters in the process of remembering some former happiness or looking forward to some future improvement in their situations. At the same time, he implies that authentic fulfillment becomes possible only when memory and expectation have been abandoned.

Vladimir introduces the theme of the happier past somewhat incongruously when he remarks that there once was a time when they could have jumped to their deaths from the Eiffel Tower: "Hand in hand from the top of the Eiffel Tower, among the first. We were respectable in those days. Now it's too late. They wouldn't even let us up" (7). Estragon similarly alludes to a brighter time in the past when their chances of happiness were not reduced to the dismal prospects that we now witness: "That's where we'll go [to the Dead Sea], I used to say, that's where we'll go for our honeymoon. We'll swim. We'll be happy" (8). Pozzo later contributes to this theme when he remarks that Lucky was once capable of feats far exceeding his present abilities: "He used to dance the farandole, the fling, the brawl, the jig, the fandango and even the hornpipe. He capered. For joy. Now that's the best he can do" (27).

Memory and Expectation

Characters' recollections of the past are complemented by their preoccupation with the future. The principal action or nonaction of the play focuses on the arrival of Godot, who, according to Vladimir, will rescue them from their present circumstances. Pozzo, no longer satisfied with the quality of Lucky's services, proposes to ease himself of his present burden by selling Lucky at a country fair. Beyond these banal expectations of future improvement, the play contains frequent allusions to the disturbing fascination that the prospect of their eventual extinction exercises on the characters. Vladimir and Estragon speak of committing suicide, an act that, in a perverse fashion, assumes the possibility of improving on the present. Estragon even attempted it once:

Estragon: Do you remember the day I threw myself into the Rhone?

Vladimir: We were grape harvesting.

Estragon: You fished me out. (35)

Estragon's failure to complete the act is a foreboding of their present difficulties: they cannot jump from the Eiffel Tower nor can they hang themselves from the tree, a feat that they try to accomplish at the end of the play.

Although references to past and future pervade the play, Beckett treats recollection and anticipation in such a way as to rob these activities of any positive significance and to imply that they prevent us from experiencing the restorative powers of the present moment. The unreliability of the past is raised by Vladimir's musings on the story of the two thieves in which he is unable to explain why there are such discrepancies in the Gospel accounts of this episode. Suspicion also surrounds the crucial past moment of their earlier meeting with Godot since they are very vague on such essential details as what they asked him and what he promised them in return:

Estragon: What exactly did we ask him for?

Vladimir: Were you not there?

Estragon: I can't have been listening.

Vladimir: Oh . . . Nothing very definite. (13)

It would be difficult to imagine a play in which a past event lends less authority to present behavior than it does in *Godot*. The play shows us two characters who, through the constant urging of one, have largely reduced the present moment to a role of servitude to a discredited past. Likewise, the future is deprived of its authority by our growing disbelief that it will bring any improvement whatsoever. We are left with the impression of a present moment that has become disfigured by the repression of its own autonomy and originality.

One of the most striking differences between Vladimir and Estragon is that the former has a much better memory; he also possesses a much greater capacity for hope. We may be inclined to think that Vladimir's more impressive possession of these faculties would imply a certain superiority on his part. It is not entirely certain, however, that Beckett himself would share this positive valuation of Vladimir's presumed virtues. In *Proust*, recalling that Proust himself had a bad memory, he launches a spirited and disdainful attack on people who possess good powers of memory. For such a person, "memory is uniform, a creature of routine, at once a condition and function of his impeccable habit, an instrument of reference instead of an instrument of discovery."[40]

This stricture against remembering should lead us to think differently of Estragon's failure to remember things and his equally decided inability to live in the expectation of some future improvement. One can understand the temptation to interpret Estragon's lapses negatively. To lose one's memory is to lose an important instrument through which we orientate ourselves within the world. However, while conscious, voluntary memory is an essential instrument of daily living, it is irrelevant to the artist's deeper purposes. Beckett implicitly agrees with Proust that "voluntary memory (Proust repeats it ad nauseam) is of no value as an instrument of evocation, and provides an image as far removed from the real as the myth of our imagination or the caricature furnished by direct perception."[41] Without elucidating all of the implications of this statement, we should at least notice that it asserts that conscious acts of remembering are incapable of evoking the essential reality of past events and cannot contribute to that quest for reality that is the artist's central concern. The artist begins to perceive reality only when he has suspended the conscious activity of remembering.

The habit of organizing perception around the acts of remembering and expecting closely resembles the habitual picturing of events in the world according to relations of cause and effect. In both cases, the ego represents the world in a way that ensures the exercise of its power. In a world structured by causality, power can hypothetically be achieved by mastering its rules so as to produce desired effects. To suspend this form of relationship, as Beckett does in *Godot*, is to pose a serious threat to the continuation of the ego's authority. Similarly, to deprive the individual of the ability to remember past promises and to look forward expectantly to their fulfillment is once again to sap the foundations on which the preeminence of the ego depends. However, in the work of a writer for whom the ego is more an adversary than an ally, this undermining of its stability should be positively welcomed. Only after the ego has been dethroned can the "smothered divinity" of unconscious experience, to which Beckett refers in *Proust*, return.

At the beginning of *Godot* one of Vladimir's first acts is, in effect, to remember who Estragon is, to impose on him the continutity of a stable ego: "So there you are again" (7). Estragon's reply, "Am I?," attacks memory and identity at its deepest foundations. It marks him as a character whose ego is not very firmly established; appropriately, he relies on the activities of remembering and expecting much less than Vladimir. We should not be too surprised that a character capable of forgetting who he is should also fail, as Estragon does in the second act, in spite of Vladimir's continual prodding, to recall events from Act I. When Estragon cannot remember details of the beating that he suffered during the night, Vladimir offers a self-congratulatory analysis of their differences whose irony escapes him: "Ah no, Gogo, the truth is there are things escape you that don't escape me, you must feel it yourself" (38). We ourselves cannot escape the feeling that Vladimir is the unwitting victim of those intact powers of memory that Beckett derides in *Proust*.

Estragon must be constantly reminded of the future event, Godot's arrival, which he would never await if left to his own devices. His capacity for recalling past events is similarly diminished. When they talk about the tree, for example, Vladimir fails to convince Estragon that yesterday they had contemplated suicide:

> *Vladimir:* Do you not remember? We nearly hanged ourselves from it. But you wouldn't. Do you not remember?
>
> *Estragon:* You dreamt it.
>
> *Vladimir:* Is it possible you've forgotten already?
>
> *Estragon:* That's the way I am. Either I forget immediately or I never forget. (39)

Vladimir then tests Estragon's recollection of the main event of the previous day, the encounter with Lucky and Pozzo:

> *Vladimir:* And Pozzo and Lucky, have you forgotten them too?
>
> *Estragon:* Pozzo and Lucky?
>
> *Vladimer:* He's forgotten everything! (39)

This exchange, as well as numerous others that are to follow, amply justify Estragon's admission that he is "no historian." Our spontaneous reaction to these moments is very likely to identify with Vladimir: we intuitively confirm the rightness of his recollection as opposed to Estragon's forgetting. Estragon is mistaken in failing to recall details that we also observed in Act I. This is no doubt true, but it misses the essential point that remembering such things is not necessarily an advantage. Beckett's own comments, in fact, encourage the contrary conclusion that memory is a source of alienation.

Vladimir's attachment to past promises and future expectations brings him no fulfillment and, in fact, imprisons him in an abstract world from which the sensual pleasures of the present moment are excluded in principle. Beckett argues in *Proust* that real happiness can be achieved only when we have freed individual moments of perception from any disfiguring context: "But when the object is perceived as particular and unique and not merely the member of a family, when it appears independent of any general notion and detached from the sanity of a cause, isolated and inexplicable in the light of ignorance, then and then only may it be a source of enchantment."[42] *Godot* is a play that, in spite of the superficial impression of incoherence, suffers from its servitude to the "sanity of a cause"—that is, Vladimir's recollection of a past promise and his expectation of its fulfillment. His repressive insistence that the present moment submit to this "general notion" makes him, for the most part, insensitive to moments that possess individual intensity rather than a definable place within a larger pattern. Hence, his indifference to the cloud to which Estragon calls his attention:

Estragon:	Look at the little cloud.
Vladimir:	*(raising his eyes).* Where?
Estragon:	There. In the zenith.
Vladimir:	Well? *(Pause.)* What is there so wonderful about it? (54)

Vladimir's indifference to the passage of the cloud—a fleeting yet nonetheless immediate and concrete image—implicitly condemns his obsession with the abstract image of the benefits that he expects from Godot. His absorption in a hypothetical, and highly dubious, future renders him insensitive to momentary sources of refreshment. He does notice the miraculous appearance of leaves on the previously barren tree, but this discovery does not induce him to abandon his vigil. Moments such as these dramatize the curious fact that hope, by encouraging us to focus our attention on absent and invisible things, diminishes our capacity for enjoyment in the present moment. The longing for things that are not there distracts attention from the things that are.

Throughout *Godot* Beckett creates a tension between the desire for absent things, whether past happiness or future expectations, and the implicit recognition that the present moment contains unsuspected potential for the production of pleasure. We notice this phenomenon especially at those moments when Vladimir and Estragon launch into verbal games. These distractions are always short-lived, yet they produce momentary happiness both in characters and members of the audience.

Another device that serves the purpose of provoking immediate pleasure is the use of stylized movement and gesture. From the point of view of the expectation that structures the play, nothing happens in *Godot:* Godot himself never comes, and his arrival is no closer at the end of the play than at the beginning. Yet in contrast to this static action, characters in the play are continually in motion. Furthermore, stage movements are tightly controlled in such a way as to create a rhythmic effect that many spectators have compared to ballet. Along with these rhythmical and pleasurable movements, Beckett also creates momentary and intensely moving visual images that compensate for the tedium created by our sense of the futile passage of time. Such images include the triptych, evoking complex associations with the figure of Christ and the two thieves, that is created when Vladimir and Estragon raise Lucky to his feet (30), and the triangular figure created at the end of each act by the moon, the tree, and the stone. The aesthetic harmony of these tableaux gives us, in the present moment, a kind of enjoyment that is not subordinated to hope or expectation. We do not obtain these pleasures because we have faithfully looked forward to them; since they are already there on stage, there is no reason to hope for their arrival. Furthermore, the play cannot tease us into wondering whether they will appear.

Estragon's response to the momentary passage of the cloud recalls Beckett's favorable mention in *Proust* of objects that have been freed from the alienating constraints normally imposed by our mental categories. These experiences are rare, according to Beckett, because of the contravening influence of habit that deprives objects of their individuality. *Godot* supports the idea that the chief impediment to happiness is the habit of hoping, of placing one's confidence in fulfillments that are dependent on time. If the play has worked on us successfully, we conclude that waiting for Godot is a futile activity not simply because he may not come but because, even if he did, his arrival would not bring anything more satisfying than the pleasures available to us in the potential fullness of the present.

Vladimir and Estragon prepare to resume their vigil.

10

Friendship

Certain details of *Godot* seem to argue in favor of friendship as one of the few, perhaps the only, value capable of withstanding the disintegrative tendencies of the play. Vladimir seems genuinely concerned for Estragon's well-being. He delivers a moving speech toward the end of the play in which he speaks of having waited "with Estragon my friend, at this place, until the fall of night" (58). He also performs certain charitable acts, such as consoling Estragon after the latter has awakened from a nightmare and, later, covering his sleeping friend with his own jacket at the risk of taking a chill himself. These acts are not negligible and seem to acquire additional moral significance when contrasted with Pozzo's indifference to Lucky's sufferings.

Although *Godot* does seem to affirm compassion as a positive virtue, Beckett's treatment of friendship itself is somewhat more skeptical. He makes clear in other contexts that the really absolute values, against which all others must be measured, are solitude and silence. He summarizes Proust's own conclusions about the superiority of solitude, its role as a necessary precondition to the creation of art, in terms suggesting that he finds this idea particularly congenial. He tells us that, for Proust, "friendship is a function of [man's] cowardice . . . the negation of that irremediable solutide to which every human being is condemned. Friendship implies an almost piteous acceptance of face values. Friendship is a social expedient, like upholstery or the distribution of garbage buckets."[43] The concluding metaphor—clearly Beckett's own since there are no garbage buckets in Proust—would seem to indicate the relish with which he is warming to his topic, that is, the dismissal of friendship as a source of positive value. Friendship arises from the fear of solitude, yet it is only through solitude that contact with the real self, obscured by social intercourse, can be restored. For Beckett, art is the "apotheosis of solitude"; for the true artist "the rejection of friendship is not only reasonable, but a necessity."

In *Godot* Beckett expresses this skeptical attitude toward friendship in two related ways: first, by exposing the egotism that often underlies ostensible acts of friendship and, second, by intimating the positive benefits to be achieved from solitude. He points our attention to the egotistical side of friendship when, at the beginning of the play, he has Vladimir boast to Estragon that if it were not for him, "You'd be nothing more than a little heap of bones at the present minute, no doubt about it" (7). Vladimir himself implicitly admits the selfish motivation underlying his apparent altruism when he abjures Estragon to join him in responding to Pozzo's cries for help: "Let us do something, while we have the chance! It is not everyday that we are needed" (51).

We may also assume that Vladimir and Estragon remain together not because of friendship in any ennobling sense of the word but simply because they are in the habit of being together. At the end of Act I, when they discuss the possibility of separating, their decision to remain together is not inspired by any strikingly positive considerations:

> *Estragon:* Wait! (*He moves away from Vladimir.*) I sometimes wonder if we wouldn't have been better off alone, each one for himself. (*He crosses the stage and sits down on the mound.*) We weren't made for the same road.
>
> *Vladimir:* (*without anger*). It's not certain.
>
> *Estragon:* No, nothing is certain.

Friendship

Vladimir slowly crosses the stage and sits down beside Estragon.

Vladimir: We can still part, if you think it would be better.

Estragon: It's not worth while now. (35)

This is a remarkably desultory conversation in which the most cogent reason for not separating seems to be the uncertain consequences of such a decision. Any favorable interpretation of their relationship is weakened by our sense that their act of remaining together is more an expression of routine than of any positive value. They have been together for so long that separation would be a rather frightening eventuality.

Skepticism about the positive value of friendship in the play should also be aroused by the suspicion that Estragon, in particular, might be better off without his friend. It is, after all, Vladimir's unrelenting insistence that they await Godot's arrival that prevents Estragon from following the prompting of his own instincts, which have at least preserved some of their original spontaneity. When he claims, gesturing toward his rags in support of his contention, that he was once a poet, we may be tempted to see a parallel between his situation and Lucky's: both have come under the sway of characters who deprive them of their autonomy without visibly giving them anything very substantive in return. The inhibitions that Vladimir imposes on Estragon, although less cruel than the control that Pozzo exercises over Lucky, nonetheless support the idea that friendships are, in part, pretexts for the exercise of power.

It is, appropriate—given Beckett's insistence that friendship is a barrier to the only project worthy of an artist's attention, the restoration of contact with that real self that is repressed by social intercourse—that the only occasions of insight in the play occur when characters are alone or at least isolated in some way from the other main characters. At these moments, they express in monologues a depth of vision and understanding largely absent from their conversations. One of the most memorable of these moments occurs at the end of the play when Vladimir, left alone after Estragon falls asleep, speaks with sudden lucidity and penetration:

Was I sleeping, while the others suffered? Am I sleeping now? To-morrow, when I wake, or think I do, what shall I say of to-day? That with Estragon my friend, at this place, until the fall of night, I waited for Godot? That Pozzo passed, with his carrier, and that he spoke to us? Probably. But in all that what truth will there be? (*Estragon, having struggled with his boots in vain, is dozing off again: Vladimir looks at him.*) He'll know nothing. He'll tell me about the blows he received and I'll give him a carrot. (*Pause.*) Astride of a grave and a difficult birth. Down in the hole, linger-ingly, the grave-digger puts on the forceps. We have time to grow old. The air is full of our cries. (*He listens.*) But habit is a great deadener. (*He looks again at Estragon.*) At me too someone is looking, of me too someone is saying, He is sleeping, he knows nothing, let him sleep on. (*Pause.*) I can't go on! (*Pause.*) What have I said? (58)

The hypnotic quality of the speech, created by its poetic imagery and cadences, reinforces our sense that this is a moment of heightened awareness. In rhythms slow, almost lulling, then images abrupt and terrifying, Beckett evokes a dreamlike state where the line between waking and sleep and all other comfortable oppositions vanish. The very reality, as well as the validity, of our conscious lives, and the stories that we tell ourselves to substantiate this sense of reality, is revealed as illusory. Death, haunting and terrible—"The gravedigger puts on the forceps"—is only a hairbreadth away from the moment of birth and, as the mixing of images implies, scarcely distinguishable from life itself. As the boundary between reassuring oppositions fades, a disquieting but lucid awareness emerges: the recognition that habit, the veil through which we perceive and construct our world, cuts us off from the deepest layers of feeling and revelation at the same time that it defends us against the suffering of others, who only too clearly perceive our sleep and self-deception.

Beyond individual points of interpretation, we also sense intu-itively that the speech itself has far more weight than anything else said by Vladimir in the course of the play. His countless exchanges with Estragon have been so much wasted breath, interminable dialogues lacking in the disabused lucidity that we find in his concluding monologue. Humankind cannot, however, bear too much reality; hence Vladimir "awakens" from his trance and attempts to dismiss the knowledge that it brought him. A moment later the arrival of Godot's messenger permits him to flee such insight by returning to his routine.

The most famous example of a monologue addressed to no one in particular, but possibly worth as much as all the rest of the dialogue in the play, is Lucky's speech. One may suspect that Lucky is entirely mute throughout the rest of the play because Beckett wanted to establish an inverse proportion between his refusal to enter the trivial world of dialogue and the profundity of the vision expressed in his great monologue. No one else in the play understands the predicament of characters as well as Lucky. He speech is not directly about himself; rather, it embraces all of humanity, which he situates between an indifferent God and an earth "abode of stones." Just before delivering himself of his speech, he performs a dance that, as Pozzo informs the other couple, he calls the Net: "The Net. He thinks he's entangled in a net" (27). Lucky is undoubtedly right, and his insistence in his speech that man is orphaned in a cruel universe is well substantiated by the play. But his monologue utters truths so damaging to the well-being of the ego that they must be violently rejected. This is precisely what happens, of course. Vladimir and Estragon, infuriated or disgusted by Lucky's tirade, finally beat him into submission; he drops in silence to the ground after declaring that his speech is "unfinished."

Not only does Lucky speak the truth in his speech, but he delivers it with an enthusiasm bordering on a kind of inspired frenzy that can be stopped only by the application of repressive force. Unlike the dialogue between Vladimir and Estragon, which is always coming to an end, defeated by the impossibility of communication and the loss of energy that it exacts, Lucky's solitary speech is self-delighting and potentially endless. Something like the upsurge of trapped energy that characterizes Lucky's speech also occurs in those moments when Estragon falls asleep on his stone. Sleeping allows Estragon to enter the world of dream, which he finds, on the evidence of his behavior on waking, far more vivid and exciting than life with Vladimir. Estragon is not, for the most part, a gifted conversationalist: he frequently does not understand what Vladimir is talking about, or doesn't really care very much, or is simply incapable of uttering the response that will keep the conversational ball rolling. Each time that he awakens, however, he must, on the contrary, be forcefully restrained from giving expression to his dreams:

> Estragon: I had a dream.
> Vladimir: Don't tell me!
> Estragon: I dreamt that—
> Vladimir: DON'T TELL ME! (11)

Estragon is prevented from expressing the details of his dream but does at least convey the superior vitality of dreams to the drab world into which he awakens. Beckett tells us in a stage direction that, after being roused by Vladimir, Estragon is "restored to the horror of his situation," as though dreaming had provided a temporary respite from the bleakness of waking life. This impression is confirmed when, after Vadimir has shouted his second refusal to listen to the dream, Estragon asks a question that points simultaneously to the superiority of our private universe and the impossibility of conveying their riches in the form of dialogue: "(gesture towards the universe). This one is enough for you? (Silence.) It's not nice of you, Didi. Who am I to tell my private nightmares to if I can't tell them to you?" (11).

Even if the content of a dream is disturbing, the unconscious impulses whose activity they restore are preferable to the tedium of waking life. Such would seem to be the conclusion implied by the nightmare that awakens Estragon in the second act:

> Estragon wakes with a start, jumps up, casts about wildly. Vladimir runs to him, puts his arms round him.) There . . . there . . . Didi is there . . . don't be afraid . . .
> Estragon: Ah!
> Vladimir: There . . . there . . . it's all over.
> Estragon: I was falling.

Friendship

Vladimir: It's all over, it's all over.

Estragon: I was on top of a—

Vladimir: Don't tell me! Come, we'll walk it off. (45)

Beckett captures with exemplary clarity in this passage the contradiction inherent in their friendship: Vladimir offers a form of security that is really the equivalent of tedium and that is offered only at the price of instinctual renunciation. We can be sure that Beckett does not share Vladimir's dismissive valuation of nightmares. In *Proust* he asserts a key idea behind his own work: the best part of ourselves remains hidden during periods of waking consciousness and returns only in privileged moments, such as when "we escape into the spacious annex of mental alienation, in sleep or the rare dispensation of waking madness."[44] There can be little doubt that, from Beckett's point of view at least, Vladimir's friendly gesture of encouraging Estragon to calm down after his nightmare is really a way of depriving him of a gift that should be positively valued.

Although our instinctive dislike of Pozzo discourages us from attributing any positive qualities to him, he is at least more interesting during his monologues than at other moments in the play. When Pozzo is speaking directly, in his own person, to other characters on stage, he has nothing worthwhile to say. He shouts orders at Lucky and imposes himself on Vladimir and Estragon with insufferable arrogance.

Certain of his monologues, however, far exceed any expectations that have been established by these details of his behavior. We may find odious his insistence on everyone's undivided attention and be similarly repelled by his melodramatic posturing, but his speech about the coming of night, for example, is both haunting and lucid. He begins by inviting the other characters to contemplate the evening sky and then continues by drawing an implied comparison between the approach of dusk and human mortality: "but behind this veil of gentleness and peace night is charging (*vibrantly*) and will burst upon us (*snaps his fingers*) pop! like that! (*his inspiration leaves him*) just when we least expect it. (*Silence. Gloomily.*) That's how it is on this bitch of an earth" (25). The defects of the speech arise from the personal faults of the speaker, but its virtues are many also. In particular, the speech does show Pozzo as capable of understanding an important truth: all of the posturing in the world cannot ultimately hide from him the recognition of his own nothingness.

Like those other moments in *Godot* in which characters achieve heightened awareness, Pozzo's speech confirms the equation between insight and solitude. Beckett accepts the convention according to which the language of a play is cast primarily in the form of dialogue. However, the most striking revelations found in *Godot* occur in monologues where language, freed from the requirements of conversation, approaches vision.

11

Family

Aristotle does not stipulate that the central action of a tragedy must focus on relations among members of a family, but playwrights have traditionally constructed their plays as though the wisdom of such a practice were self-evident. The tragedy in *Oedipus Rex* depends on the existence of a mother and father on whom Oedipus can perform the interdicted acts. The dramatic tension of *Antigone* would be lost if there were no family whose rights can be opposed to the competing authority of the state. The tragic action of *Hamlet* and *King Lear* also evolves from decisions that are based on obedience to, or refusal of, obligations that arise within the context of familial relationships. Even such twentieth-century experimental plays as Luigi Pirandello's *Six Characters in Search of an Author* or Bertolt Brecht's *Mother Courage* do not depart from this traditional reliance on the family to provide the essential forms of relationships among individual characters.

There is, however, no family in *Godot*. Its absence is even more striking when the play is compared with other works that Beckett was writing at about the same time. The unpublished play "Eleutheria," for example, deals with materials drawn from Beckett's own life, particularly his troubled relationship with his mother. The main character, Victor Krapp, a thinly disguised representative of Beckett himself, is struggling to escape the oppressive dominance of his mother; his situation, like Beckett's own, is rendered even more desperate by the death of his father, who, in spite of his ineffectiveness, was nevertheless sympathetic to Victor's difficulties.

Similarly, in *Molloy*, the novel that Beckett wrote one year before *Godot*, familial relations receive central emphasis. The first part of the novel recounts the narrator's failed effort to return to his mother, which, as he admits at one point, has been the single aim of his entire life; the second part deals with the paternal pole of the parental fixation. Its narrator, Jacques Moran, wants both to satisfy the demands made on him by a paternal figure named Youdi and to be respected and admired by his own son. In both "Eleutheria" and *Molloy* we notice the same configuration, formed on the one hand by an obsessive, and even pathological, attachment to parental figures and, on the other, by an intense yearning to escape the paralyzing effects of these attachments.

When we turn from these contemporaneous works to *Godot*, we are first struck by the fact that there is no mother in the play. Beckett has also consistently refused permission to any director wanting to have one of the roles played by an actress. The most recent of these refusals occurred in the fall of 1987 when he rejected a request from the director of the first production of *Godot* ever to be allowed in East Germany.

There has been some speculation that women are excluded from *Godot* because Beckett was horrified by the idea of having to deal with an actress during rehearsals of the play. There may also be some truth in the related hypothesis that banishing not only mothers but familial relationships in their totality constitutes a form of wish fulfillment. If, in effect, the family has disappeared, perhaps it can no longer exercise the blighting effect on personality with which it is so frequently accused elsewhere in Beckett's work.

Although Beckett jettisons the family in *Godot*, we do hear allusions to this otherwise missing institution several times in the play. The image of the married couple is evoked, though in comically distorted form, by Estragon's improbable remark while describing pictures of the Holy Land: "That's where we'll go, I used to say, that's where we'll go for our honeymoon" (8). Toward the end of Act I Estragon echoes another kind of conjugal sentiment when he tells Vladimir: "I sometimes wonder if we wouldn't have been better off alone, each one for himself" (35).

Although references to sexuality do occur in *Godot*, they are isolated from the context of the heterosexual ccouple as well as from the theme of the regeneration of life. A brief allusion to the divorce between sexuality and regeneration appears in the anecdote of the Englishman in the brothel, which Estragon wants Vladimir to recount. Sexual potency is referred to only once in the play, when Vladimir and Estragon contemplate the possibility of suicide:

Estragon: What about hanging ourselves?

Vladimir: Hmm. It'd give us an erection.

Estragon: (*highly excited*). An erection!

Vladimir: With all that follows. Where it falls mandrakes grow. That's why they shriek when you pull them up. (12)

The incompleteness of Vladimir's description of "all that follows" underlines the curiously truncated treatment of sexuality in the play. We may further suspect that the significance of the two episodes in which Vladimir leaves the stage to urinate (in one instance he is rather improbably cheered on by Estragon as though he were accomplishing an admirable feat) is that they suggest the diminished potency of the virile member. Like the mother's sexual organ in Pozzo's later illusion to birth astride the grave, the phallus, emphatically deprived of any positive, life-giving significance, is exclusively associated with enfeeblement, sterility, and death.

Having displaced sexual difference and the procreative function of the couple from the center of *Godot*, allowing it only peripheral appearances in fragmented and distorted form, Beckett also deprives relationships between successive generations of the importance traditionally assigned to them. Not only are the four main characters of the same sex; they also belong to the same generation, Estragon's guess about Lucky's age notwithstanding:

> Pozzo: (*To Vladimir.*) What age are you, if it's not a rude question? (*Silence.*) Sixty? Seventy? (*To Estragon.*) What age would you say he was?
>
> Estragon: Eleven. (19)

That distinctions of generation are, along with sexual distinctions, a constant point of reference in real life is alluded to only in a marginal way in *Godot*. The four main characters are perhaps younger than Godot, if indeed he exists and has a white beard. The only undeniable allusion to differences between generations occurs when Godot's messenger, who is decidedly younger than anyone else we have seen to this point, arrives on stage.

Although the literal family, within whose context differences of sex and generation are first learned, is granted only fragmentary representation in *Godot*, something like the family does nonetheless return through symbolic details of the play. There is no real mother in *Godot*, or even a woman who could potentially become a mother, but the maternal function itself emerges through the ancient association of the mother with the earth. This relationship is made explicit at several points in the play. Pozzo, for example, concludes his monologue on mortality and the inevitability of death with the observation, "That's how it is on this bitch of an earth" (25). In Act II, when all four major characters are lying on the ground, Estragon evokes this association through his appreciative apostrophe to "sweet mother earth" (25). Probably the most famous of the allusions occurs when Pozzo speaks of mothers who "give birth astride of a grave," a grotesque version of the traditional womb/tomb analogy that Vladimir develops in his concluding speech: "Astride of a grave and a difficult birth. Down in the hole, lingeringly, the grave-digger puts on the forceps" (58).

Like the mother, the father is absent as a human character in *Godot* but reappears in symbolic form. The association between Godot and the paternal function is established at several points in the play. In response to Vladimir's question regarding Godot's physical appearance, the young boy who serves as his messenger replies that Godot has a white beard, a disquieting detail since, as Vladimir's fearful reaction implies, it associates him with the paternal God of the Old Testament, a connection that is reinforced when the boy tells Vladimir that he minds the goats and his brother has been given charge of the sheep. The divine aspect of Godot is further underlined by the fact that he never appears in the play in embodied form and that on several occasions when the obligation of awaiting his arrival is mentioned, Vladimir and Estragon look in a gesture of silent expectation to the sky, as though it were Godot's abode. It is also worth remarking the tremendous power exercised by the mere mention of Godot's name. Like the Old Testament God, Godot's existence is "proved" not by the physical evidence of the senses but by the abstractions of language. He has made a verbal promise, and it is through a repeated verbal reminder that Vladimir persuades Estragon to continue waiting.

The physical space of the play, the plot of ground on which Vladimir and Estragon are standing, also represents paternal authority in the sense that Godot has designated it as the spot where the anticipated meeting will take place. The land, having lost its maternal function of nurturing, has been transformed into a setting where the father exercises his power of eliciting obedient actions from his subjects.

The disappearance of the literal family and its replacement by fragmentary or symbolic allusions can be interpreted in several ways. To begin with, Beckett may be depriving the family of its traditional prominence while dramatizing the persistence of its crippling effects. Even without a literal mother or father in the play, the enfeeblement of Vladimir and Estragon nonetheless dramatizes the situation of children who are utterly dependent on a parent: they cannot oblige the earth to nurture them, nor can they require that Godot keep his promise. The failure of these symbolic parental figures to fulfill their functions, as well as Vladimir and Estragon's inability to escape from their dependency, may suggest the persistence into adult life of frustrations and patterns of behavior first acquired in infancy.

A second line of interpretation follows from the observation that, in the absence of the family, relationships among characters in the play are based largely on power and economic realities. This is so blatant in the case of the relationship between Pozzo and Lucky as scarcely to warrant further comment. Lucky is not an irreplaceable individual, as he would be from the point of view the family; rather, as Pozzo makes clear, he is an economic unit who, having outlived his usefulness, will now be sold at whatever price the market will offer, to be then replaced by another servant who will himself eventually become a disposable.

The same pattern can be found in the relationship that ties Vladimir and Estragon to Godot. We never discover why Godot continues to deceive the couple as to his real intentions, but we do know that they continue waiting for him because they expect him to render them a desirable service. Their compliance with his directives, whether it arouses our sympathy or contempt, follows from their self-interested calculations: if only they persist in waiting long enough, so Vladimir's reasoning goes, perhaps they will eventually gain something in terms of material benefits.

Traditional plays, using the familial model that is dismissed in *Godot*, often focus on the passage of power from parents to children, as well as the complications, whether comic or tragic, to which this may lead. Beckett, however, has created in *Godot* a world that is more managerial than familial. Those characters who lack power may, at best, hope for some meager improvement in their situation. Unlike sons or daughters in traditional plays, however, they can never hope to inherit power since the passage of an inheritance from one generation to the next is ruled out in principle.

An example of Beckett's treatment of this theme in his prose fiction occurs in his second novel, *Watt,* in which the main character goes to work for a Godot-like character named Mr. Knott. Mr. Knott's establishment is described in such a way as to emphasize its resemblance to a modern bureaucracy: workers are highly stratified, each having his own limited powers and responsibilities; few of them have direct access to Mr. Knott himself; furthermore, all of these workers are interchangeable and eventually disposable.

This would seem a rather conventional representation of a bureaucratized society were it not for the curious fact that Mr. Knott's establishment is referred to not as a business firm or a corporation but as a "house." In other words the setting of the novel arises from the superimposition of two settings that we normally assume to be antithetical or at least to occupy different physical spaces. Beckett sets a considerable part of his novel in a house—a place where we expect to find parents and children. He then subverts this expectation by giving us, instead, servants of varying ranks and a character who rules them not as a father, who eventually is required to relinquish power to the next generation, but rather as a quasi-immortal tyrant who presides indifferently over the arrivals and departures of his underlings.

Having dismissed the family as its central structuring principle, *Godot* likewise dramatizes relationships based exclusively on differences in power rather than on the sexual and generational distinctions by which the family is defined. Its implicit representation of a real world in which power, no longer transmitted from one generation to the next, remains the perpetually elusive prerogative of an unattainable ruler, is the key to the play's sociopolitical interest.

A third kind of interpretation relates the disappearance of the family to the subversion of language in the play. Language and the family are interdependent means through which we discover our identity and our place in the world. Just as what James Joyce called the "legal fiction" of paternity can be established only through language, so also does language articulate those complex relationships within the family triangle that allow the child to discover who he is.

In *Godot* language offers only inept or discredited orderings of the world. Statements are begun but are not completed because a failure of memory intervenes. Other phrases are uttered repeatedly without being understood or without influencing the action of the play. Conversely, those moments that illustrate the effectiveness of language are generally those that make communication synonymous with brutality and violence.

This simultaneous subversion of language and the family allows the foregrounding of relationships that are physical rather than verbal or familial. Language does not add much to our understanding of the basic parameters of Vladimir and Estragon's relationship. One of the few occasions when language intervenes to define their relationship occurs toward the end of the play when Vladimir refers to Estragon as "my friend," a relationship that we would have deduced even if we were watching the play in a language that we did not understand. The one other occasion when a human relationship is specified by language occurs when Pozzo tells Estragon and Vladimir that Lucky is his "knook," a verbal clue that neither characters nor members of the audience find especially illuminating.

The essential facts about the couple are conveyed with admirable clarity and precision by physical gesture and movement: Estragon has foot trouble and falls asleep a lot; something is wrong with Vladimir's groin and, unlike the somnolent Estragon, he is always on the alert. Like most friends, their relationship is a complicated mixture of affection and dependence—conveyed by moments in which they embrace, dance together, or organize a little promenade around the stage—and dislike or even repugnance, conveyed to us by equally forceful and unambiguous physical gestures. The distinctions between the two characters are dramatized through spatial relationships: one sits on a stone, whereas the other spends a good deal of time walking around. Sometimes they stand close to each other; at other times, they are as far apart as the physical limits of stage permit.

If the identity of the couple largely loses its verbal and sexual dimension, returning us to a world structured by spatial relationships, something equivalent happens to the family triangle. It has been noted that the maternal and paternal figures who are absent from the play as individuals nonetheless return in symbolic form. The family triangle is subjected to yet a further displacement in the theatrical space of the play. This highly geometrical space is dominated by the figure of the triangle, which has been purified of all symbolic meaning, oedipal or otherwise. There are three principal manifestations of this figure: the first formed by the stone, the tree, and the stool; the second by the stone, Lucky, and the stool; and the third by the stone, the moon, and the tree.

These triangles are not symbols of anything; rather, they form a concrete visual form that is completely liberated from meaning. As pure shapes they return us to a stage of consciousness that precedes the acquisition of language and the alienating discovery of our place within the familial triangle. They are also liberated from the rigidity of the family triangle because they are constantly dispersing and reforming. Their fluidity contrasts with the stasis of the "symbolic" family that inhabits the play. As a further contrast, there is nothing repressive about the functioning of these triangles: they impose neither obligations nor limits. Characters may move whenever they want to and may occupy any point on the stage. Although the symbolic familial triangle dramatizes the frustration of desire, the continuously evolving concrete triangles offer us release from these constraints. For Vladimir and Estragon, satisfaction is endlessly deferred; for members of the audience, it is constantly present through the concrete shapes created by their stylized movements.

The disappearance of the family triangle in *Godot* and its return in two anithetical forms—one symbolic, the other concrete—lead logically to two opposing conclusions. On the one hand, the symbolic reappearance intensifies the play's pessimism with regard to the future: not only is Godot unlikely to appear but, more important, Vladimir and Estragon will remain permanently trapped within the alienating system of relationships imposed by the family, endlessly condemned to interpreting the world in terms of their inevitably frustrated needs for nurturing and protection. On the other hand, Beckett does seem to suggest, through the deployment of concrete, nonsignifying triangles, that escape from the alienating structures of language and family can be achieved. As we listen to the words of the play, we often hear repeated a story of frustration and deprivation. However, as we watch the rhythmical unfolding of formal spatial relations produced by objects and characters on stage, we experience intimations of release.

The triangular space of the stage.

12

Visual Form

Almost everyone who has seen productions of *Godot* staged by Beckett himself or by directors who have worked closely with him has remarked on the importance of physical movement and gesture to the aesthetic effect of the play. Several have described Beckett's approach to the staging of *Godot* as "choreographic," and Beckett himself has substantiated this metaphor by underlining the importance of what he calls "form in movement." Although the unfolding of dramatic action has been largely excluded from *Godot*, the play is nonetheless replete with rhythmical movements. The immediate delight that they provoke replaces the deferred pleasure of awaiting some eventual fulfillment.

One of the principal examples of rhythmical movement in the play is created by Vladimir and Estragon's repeated gesture of union and separation, what Beckett calls in his production notebook their "perpetual moving apart and coming together again." This alternating rhythm is echoed in one of Lucky's pantomimes: "*Lucky sags slowly, until bag and basket touch the ground, then straightens up with a start and begins to sag again*" (17). Yet another rhythmical opposition arises from the constant tension between movement and stasis in the play. Characters suddenly begin gesticulating with exceptional expressive force and then just as suddenly revert to immobility. Certain movements alternate with snatches of dialogue; at other times, characters speak while moving and come to a halt when they fall silent.

Along with rhythmical movements based on the binary oppositions of union and separation or movement and stasis, Beckett also underscores in his notebooks the importance of movements that unfold in three phases. Vladimir and Estragon's approach to Lucky (17), for example, requires three distinct movements: the first is stopped by the question, "What ails him?" and the second by "Careful!"; the third brings them finally face to face. Similarly, the arrival of Godot's messenger at the center of the stage (32) is marked by three phases. He passes the tree with Vladimir's "Approach, my child," moves a bit closer when Estragon shouts, "Approach when you're told, can't you," and comes to a halt at the center after Estragon's "Will you approach!"

The rhythmical movement of *Godot* is crucial to its effect, as Beckett's detailed attention to this aspect of his play indicates. It serves as one of the principal means through which he implies that *Godot* is not only about the act of waiting. The main action of the play is truncated in the sense that it lacks a satisfying conclusion. The rhythms of the play, however, whether produced by binary oppositions or tripartite progressions, are perfectly complete: they do not lack anything, nor could they be improved by the addition of further elements. Hence, the movement of *Godot* offers in abundance those fulfillments that are denied to the action of the play.

In addition to possessing distinctive and aesthetically pleasing rhythms, the play's movement is also highly geometrical. We notice, for example, that Vladimir and Estragon move from one point to another by describing a semicircle, rather than walking directly to their destination. Likewise, when Pozzo first appears he walks around the stage in a sweeping circle, later echoed by Vladimir and Estragon when they circle around Lucky. At other times, an unnatural rigidity in characters' way of walking emphasizes the perfect straightness of the lines described by their movements. Rectangularity is indicated several times when characters walk to the extreme limits of the stage, suggesting the idea of their entrapment within an enclosed space. Beckett underlines the importance of this particular figure when he says in his production notebook that the movement of characters should imply that they are in a cage.

The most persistent geometrical figure in *Godot*, discernible from the opening scene and undergoing innumerable transformations throughout the play, is the triangle. The evolution of this figure is accomplished in logically rigorous steps. Before the dialogue between Vladimir and Estragon begins, our attention is drawn along the diagonal line that runs from the stone (downstage right) to the tree (upstage left). Estragon reinforces our awareness of this line when, several minutes later, he rises from his stone and walks diagonally toward the tree.

When Vladimir first appears, he is strictly limited to moving back and forth along the apron of the stage: a constraint that has no realistic purpose but that serves to inscribe a horizontal line on the scenic space. As the dialogue continues, Beckett, again in the absence of any logical necessity, has Vladimir and Estragon move vertically from the extreme upstage to extreme downstage positions, a movement that completes the introduction of the three distinct kinds of lines—diagonal, horizontal, and vertical—out of which he constructs his triangles. We may detect the presence of this figure as early as Vladimir's arrival. His constant back and forth movement along the apron creates a triangular shape formed in part by the stone and tree, which serve as fixed points, and in part by Vladimir himself, who serves as the third, mobile, point.

The dimension of height is added to the scenic space of *Godot*, first, by the contrasting elevations of the tree and the stone: this configuration is then reproduced by the often repeated contrast between Estragon sitting on his stone and Vladimir standing at various places on the stage (Lucky later introduces an intermediate position into this figure by adopting a hunched posture). This effect is further strengthened by the several times that Estragon falls asleep on his stone, a gesture that is clearly contrasted with those moments when Vladimir looks intently upward to the sky. Beckett has his actor adopt this position, for example, during the entirety of the dialogue on page 11. This stylized evocation of upward movement is echoed in later details of the play. After Vladimir and Estragon huddle together (13), they look to the sky when Vladimir offers the suggestion that the frightening offstage noises they have heard may have been Godot shouting at his horse. Pozzo prefaces his discourse on the coming of night by instructing his listeners to look upward. In Act II, while all four characters are lying on the stage, Estragon calls Vladimir's attention to a cloud, not only verbally but by raising his arm to the vertical position. Aside from their relation to an immediate context, these gestures all emphasize the visual geometry of *Godot*'s scenic space.

The geometrical configuration of the play becomes more complex when Pozzo and Lucky appear. We may suspect from what we have already observed that they will not be allowed to move about the stage in an arbitrary manner. The most striking consequence of the restrictions that Beckett imposes on them is that even though the number of chracters on stage has increased to four, the three-sided figure becomes an even more dominant element of the play's visual form. He creates this pattern by having Pozzo place his stool downstage, but at a point as far as possible from Estragon's stone, forming for the duration of his presence on stage a triangle composed of stone, tree, and stool. Beckett then forms an additional triangle by having Lucky and Pozzo stand at two points that are some distance from each other, while having Vladimir and Estragon stand close together at a third spot. Throughout the time that Lucky and Pozzo are on stage, a certain physical, as opposed to dramatic or psychological, tension is created by the asymmetrical presence of two triangles: the irregular triangle formed by Estragon's stone, the tree, and Pozzo's stool and the isosceles triangle formed by stone, stool, and Lucky, who usually stands in the center of the stage, equally distant from these two objects.

The concluding and perhaps the most aesthetically satisfying triangular configuration occurs at the end of each act with the sudden apparition of the moon. Until now the objects that have entered into the play's geometry have all been near at hand. Suddenly, however,

Beckett expands our field of vision by introducing an extraterrestrial object. Triangulation, which had until this moment been limited to the enclosed, earthbound space of the stage, assumes the final form of a cosmic tableau formed by the moon, the tree, and the stone.

The elaboration of a scenic space dominated by such geometrical figures as the triangle serves several purposes in *Godot*. The constantly shifting shapes of these figures is a dynamic response to the static action of the play. Although *Godot* is not terribly exciting from the point of view of dramatic action, it begins making a powerful impact on us when we become aware of the geometrical patterns that are evolving before our eyes. At such times, the boredom into which our expectation of traditional action has led us is replaced by a fascination with the aesthetic effect that this "form in movement" creates. The pleasure of watching these forms and their variations completely belies the message that there is "nothing to be done." There is not a moment in *Godot* when the actors are not contributing, in ways that make exceptional demands on their virtuosity, to the creation of remarkably complex and moving formal patterns. The impact of these visual forms diminishes our regret that Godot has not appeared.

A releated consequence of the prominence given to geometrical figures is that it tends to shift attention away from the presumed deeper meanings of the play and toward relationships among its surface elements. Beckett conveys a serious idea in comic form when, in reply to Vladimir's complaint, "This is becoming really insignificant," he has Estragon assure his partner, "Not enough" (44). He implicitly suggests in *Godot* that we must free ourselves from the tyranny of meaning in order to reinvigorate our diminished responsiveness to pure, nonsymbolic forms. The verbal language of the play requires that we know the meanings of its words, as well as its syntactical rules, in order to interpret what is being said. The physical language of *Godot*, however, communicates to a preverbal region of the psyche in which, long before we acquire words, we perceived the world in terms of shapes without bothering to ask their meanings.

The geometrical figures serve, in effect, to diminish the role of interpretation in *Godot*. Although meanings can be attributed to visual elements of the play, they have only a precarious status. The text of the play, for example, alludes to the ancient association of earth and sky with mother and father, but we are not required to regard this symbolism as anything more than a fiction, a creation of language that burdens the concrete world with abstract meanings.

Beckett's use of geometry also undermines the symbolic associations of the setting of *Godot*. Certain details of this setting may remind us of the Garden of Eden; we could interpret the tree as the Tree of Knowledge of Good and Evil as well as the cross on which Christ died; perhaps we are tempted to interpret the stone as a symbol of death or as the rock on which Christ built his church; the country road may evoke the idea of life as a journey. However, Beckett's direction of the play suggests that these meanings are not central for him. The tree and rock are more important as geometrical points than as symbols; their encrusted meanings count for less than their usefulness in shaping the scenic space of *Godot*. Although the plot of ground on which they are standing is the place where they are to meet Godot and also, according to Pozzo, land that belongs to him, geometry deprives the ground of these meanings and associations and transforms it simply into a space in which certain visual patterns are created.

The rigorous geometry of Beckett's production is also one of the principal means through which the author distances us from the human situation that is being enacted on stage. As we watch the play, we respond to its human drama, sympathizing with Vladimir and Estragon or feeling irritated by the boredom that their behavior provokes in us. In either case, we assume that their predicament is the central interest of the play. Once we have perceived the evolving geometrical patterns, however, we realize that this human drama is, in a sense, quite peripheral to the play: it serves as the point of departure for the elaboration of spatial forms that are independent of Vladimir and Estragon's predicament and are indifferent to the ultimate outcome of their expectations. Their movements and gestures, intended to express their immediate predicament, become absorbed in a higher formal pattern. The effect of watching the play is not entirely unlike the experience of watching a slowly turning mobile by Alexander Calder in which the meaning of the experience is simply in the pleasure of watching the constantly varying relationships among individual elements. The least successful versions of *Godot* are those that focus attention exclusively on such thematic elements as alienation, hopelessness, and solitude. The best are those that, through stylization, create an alternative world into which the human concerns of the play have been permitted only limited entry.

It is also important to notice that the visual form of *Godot*, which draws our attention away from the thematic center of the play, is itself a decentered space. The two fixed points of stone and tree are both off-center. Hence the dominant feature of the setting is not some central object around which the movement of the actors is organized, but the diagonal line formed by the stone and the tree and the continuously evolving triangles that they help to compose. We would expect that the space left vacant by the tree and the stone would be frequently, and for long periods, occupied by the actors. But this expectation is not to be satisfied. Until Pozzo and Lucky arrive, the center of the stage is virtually ignored. Estragon pauses there briefly—and, in defiance of traditional practice, with his back to the audience—before uttering his appreciation of the surroundings, "Charming spot" (10). Vladimir stands there for about five seconds, while Estragon is falling asleep on his stone (11). A moment later, after Vladimir has run offstage to urinate, Estragon moves to the center, where he pantomimes encouragement to his partner.

With extremely few and brief exceptions, Vladimir and Estragon stand everywhere on the stage but at the center. The words of the play force our attention in the direction of Godot, who becomes in this way a central, as well as an alienating, preoccupation of the text, but the visual form of the play generates the opposite movement: a liberating dispersal of attention that is no longer organized around the repressive domination of a center, whether thematic or physical.

Beckett's disregard for the prominence traditionally accorded to the center of the stage continues with the arrival of Lucky and Pozzo. As his bullying personality leads us to expect, Pozzo immediately occupies the position that Vladimir and Estragon have largely avoided. However, he occupies this space only for a short time. Soon, he will move downstage left where, having seated himself on his stool, he is to remain for most of his time on stage. Beckett further disrupts traditional expectations as to how the center of the stage will be used by giving it over nearly entirely to Lucky, a character who, with one memorable exception, never speaks. We are at first surprised to see a mere servant standing in the center of the stage: no traditional play provides a precedent for this unexpected practice. Lucky's standing in this position would seem to dramatize the fact that *Godot* attaches greater importance to physical gesture than to words. Traditionally, a character will stand in the center of the stage when he has something important to say. But in a play in which the communicative function of language is so devalued, it is not entirely surprising that the promotion of concrete stage language should be signified by the prominence granted to the one character most liberated from words. Lucky deserves the center because of the exceptional expressive power of his movements and gestures: one recalls in particular the extended pantomime through which he sags to the ground under the weight of his bags, returns to the erect position, sags again, and so forth and the dance, which he calls "The Net" and which comes at least as close to the truth of their situation as any of the words spoken by other characters.

Lucky's presence at the center of the stage contributes further to the effect of decentering achieved by the visual form of *Godot*. Beckett's decision to place him there, like his creation of geometrical forms throughout the play, suggests the disappearance of a traditional center and the exploration of preverbal regions of the psyche that existed before the advent of meaning and whose most appropriate expressive medium is concrete movement rather than words.

13

Metaphor and Metonymy

Beckett once told Alan Schneider that he if had known who Godot was he would have said so in the play, a comment that has given *Godot* the reputation of being such an enigmatic play that even its author cannot explain it. He later made a very different kind of statement to Walter Asmus, his assistant director for the Schiller Theater production of *Godot*, which deserves wider currency as its restores to the play some of the accessibility that it lost as a result of the better-known comment. In explaining to Asmus his vision of Vladimir and Estragon, Beckett said, "Estragon is on the ground, he belongs to the stone. Vladimir is light, he is oriented towards the sky. He belongs to the tree." Significantly, Beckett expressed his conception of these characters not by analyzing their behavior or revealing what they were meant to symbolize but by showing how he visualized their relationships with other concrete elements of the play. His comment makes clear, once again, that what concerns him is not the hidden meanings of his play but the patterns of relationship among its surface elements.

The preceding chapter indicated that the visual elements of *Godot* form mobile geometrical configurations that draw our attention to the concrete surfaces rather than to the abstract depths of the play. A different kind of pattern is suggested by the affirmation that Estragon belongs to the stone and that Vladimir is light. The relationships that Beckett implies by his remark are not geometrical; they do, however, have very clear affinities with the poetic figures of metaphor and metonymy.

Metaphor is a figure of speech that asserts a relationship of resemblance or identity between two otherwise different things. Estragon employs a metaphor, for example, when he tells Vladimir that "people are bloody ignorant apes" (9), a statement that invites us to grasp similarities between two strikingly different things. Later in the play, Vladimir introduces a more surprising metaphor when he criticizes Lucky for "crucifying" Pozzo (23), a comparison that unites two figures, Christ and Pozzo, who are otherwise widely separated from each other.

Metonymy indicates a relationship based not on resemblance but on contiguity: one object becomes a metonym of another when it exists in the same space as this object. Vladimir and Estragon produce a series of metonyms when they list the people whom Godot will consult before granting their wish:

Vladimir:	Consult his family.
Estragon:	His friends.
Vladimir:	His agents.
Estragon:	His correspondants.
Vladimir:	His books.
Estragon:	His bank account. (13)

The separate elements of this series are related not so much by resemblance as by contiguity; they all exist within a spatial realm also occupied by Godot. They "belong to" him, to use Beckett's phrase, and evoke his image through a process of association.

The text of *Godot* contains many examples of both poetic figures. When Vladimir says that the day is "very near the end of its repertory," our comprehension of this metaphoric statement depends on our grasping the implied comparison between the passage of time and a theatrical performance. Similarly when Estragon quizzes Vladimir about whether they are "tied" to Godot, he wants to know whether their obligations to him can be likened metaphorically to a physical constraint; later, when Lucky arrives with a rope tied around his neck, we recognize that the poetic comparison has been made literal. The significance of Lucky's dance likewise is expressed by a metaphor:

> *Pozzo:*   Do you know what he calls it?
> *Estragon:*   The Scapegoat's Agony.
> *Vladimir:*   The Hard Stool.
> *Pozzo:*   The Net. He thinks he's entangled in a net. (27)

Death enters the play on several occasions through metaphor. Pozzo expresses its horror and finality by comparing death to the sudden coming of night: "night is charging (*vibrantly*) and will burst upon us (*snaps his fingers*) pop! like that!" (25); toward the end of the play Vladimir deepens the grotesqueness of Pozzo's affirmation that women "give birth astride of a grave" by likening grave-diggers metaphorically to doctors: "Down in the hole, lingeringly, the grave-digger puts on the forceps" (58). Likewise, one of the most powerful effects of the language of the play is produced when Vladimir and Estragon propose a series of resonant metaphors to describe the sound of "the dead voices":

> *Vladimir:*   They make a noise like wings.
> *Estragon:*   Like leaves.
> *Vladimir:*   Like sand.
> *Estragon:*   Like leaves. . . .
> *Vladimir:*   They make a noise like feathers.
> *Estragon:*   Like leaves.
> *Vladimir:*   Like ashes.
> *Estragon:*   Like leaves. (40)

This passage illustrates the essential features of metaphoric statements. They affirm the underlying identity of objects that are clearly different from the point of view of ordinary perception, creating in this way a centripetal movement that draws together things that are distant from each other. By asserting the unity of disparate things they reveal the existence of a pattern that we would not otherwise have seen.

Examples of metonymy appear in several of the verbal games played by Vladimir and Estragon, in which they combine words belonging to the same semantic space. When, for example, they decide to insult each other, they produce a series of words: "Moron! . . . Vermin! . . . Abortion! . . . Morpion!" (48) that exist within phonetic proximity of each other. Their discussion of exercises that they might perform (49) produces a list organized the same principle of contiguity. The most impressive example of metonymy in *Godot*, however, belongs to Lucky, who spews forth the following combination, each of whose elements belongs, as he indicates himself, to the semantic space of "sports of all sorts": "the practice of sports such as tennis football running cycling swimming flying floating riding gliding conating camogie skating tennis of all kinds dying flying sports of all sorts" (29). This list is more metonymic than metaphoric because it displaces attention from one object to another while remaining within the same semantic space. We do not have to pause to wonder why football belongs to the same list as tennis because we immediately see that they are both parts of one inclusive category. Metaphor, on the other hand, does require additional thought because it condenses or merges semantic spaces—dead voices and feathers, for example—that are normally separated.

Returning to Beckett's comment to Walter Asmus, the relationships that he attributes to characters and objects in *Godot* implies the existence in the play of physical patterns like those created by metaphor and metonymy. Estragon, the stone, and the ground belong to the same space: he spends a good deal of time sitting on the stone, and his posture when he falls asleep brings him nearly into contact with the ground. The visual image that these three elements combine to form possesses that quality of physical proximity that is one of the characteristics of metonymy. Similarly, Vladimir "belongs to the tree" because he frequently stands near to it; furthermore, his standing against the rear wall intensifies this relationship since the tree is also placed against this wall. Our eye, moving from Vladimir to the tree and back again, classifies them as occupying the same space and attributes to them an implicit, metonymic relationship. On the other hand, the connection that Beckett establishes between Vladimir and light seems to be metaphoric. Vladimir does not occupy the same space as the light; rather, he resembles it in some way. He does not belong to the light; he is light, an assertion that implies an underlying identity between two things that we normally classify as belonging to quite different semantic spaces.

As we examine these relationships more closely, however, we discover that the distinction between metaphor and metonomy becomes blurred: metonymic connections possess metaphoric overtones and vice versa. Estragon, for example, does not simply sit on the stone: he actually resembles it in certain ways. His sluggishness and immobility suggest the possibility of comparison, which is confirmed when, adopting the fetal position as he falls asleep, he assumes a shape having definite visual analogies with the stone. A similar copresence of poetic figures may be noticed with respect to Vladimir and the tree. His tall angularity, along with the fact that he is usually standing throughout the play, creates a certain physical resemblance that is reinforced by the several times that he looks toward the sky, a movement that reproduces the upward thrust of the tree. Vladimir's association with the sky through his numerous glances in its direction also raises the possibility that Beckett's identifying him with light, which we immediately perceive as metaphoric, also contains a metonymic component: his looking skyward suggests, in effect, that he does indeed "belong to" the region of light as much as Estragon to his stone.

The copresence of metaphor and metonymy may also be detected in other relationships between objects and characters. Estragon's shoes are metonyms of himself: they belong to his space and become identified with him through a process of association. When the second act begins, even though Estragon is not physically present on the stage, we sense intuitively that he is represented metonymically by his shoes, which he placed on the apron of the stage at the end of Act I. His shoes also serve a metaphoric function, however, in that they evoke the ancient comparison of life to a journey. So also, Vladimir's hat is a metonymy of its owner: an object belonging to him that he is continually taking off and examining. It is also metaphoric, however, because it represents Vladimir's "intellectual" nature. Likewise, the things that characters eat during the play are all metonymies belonging to the larger semantic category food, but Beckett also assigns to them the further metaphoric function of representing the very different economic conditions that distinguish Vladimir and Estragon from Pozzo. Pozzo eats cooked chicken served to him by his slave, while Vladimir has only a carrot and a radish for Estragon.

Sometimes these connections between characters and objects are intensified by details of action. This happens, for example, when Vladimir, having returned to the stage after urinating, pushes Lucky aside and kicks over Pozzo's stool. Although not an act of monumental significance, Vladimir's act of aggression does call attention to the poetic identification between Pozzo and his stool. A second example occurs after Estragon and Vladimir have beaten Lucky to the ground, bringing his monologue to an end. While Lucky is still lying crumpled on the stage, Pozzo walks to his hat, lying not far from him on the stage, and stamps on it. The forward movement of the play is not helped in any way by this action, but it underlines once again the prominence given to poetic relationships in *Godot*. It reminds us that, from the point of view of poetic logic, the hat *is* Lucky: to crumple it is to inflict aggression on Lucky himself, a point that Pozzo underscores by his triumphant assertion, "There's an end to his thinking!" (30).

The use of verbal and scenic images based on metaphor and metonymy is not unique to *Godot*: examples of both poetic figures can be found in the most conventional play. What distinguishes *Godot*, however, is that these figures have become a fundamental structuring principle of the play, replacing the traditional reliance on relationships organized by cause and effect. Rather than showing us events that evolve in time, Beckett calls our attention to patterns that manifest themselves in space. In place of an emphasis on the unfolding of dramatic action, we have the revelation of poetic figures within the spatial form of the play.

Metonymy gives shape to the scenic space by underlining associations among contiguous objects, showing connections, for example, between Pozzo and the objects that surround him. Metaphor affects our response to the spatial dimension of the play by creating an overlap between distinct things, condensing them into composite figures by merging Estragon with his stone. Hence, the promotion of poetic over dramatic values in *Godot* is also experienced as a victory of space over time. As with the geometrical figures, we are not concerned so much with what might happen as we are with what does happen at the present moment within the scenic space of the play. The expectation of some future happiness gives way to the immediate perception of an atemporal pattern that is freed from the uncertainties that time introduces into *Godot*.

The creation of patterned relationships among characters and objects in *Godot* also requires that we revise the traditional hierarchy that places words above things. Beckett shows that we do not need verbal language in order to perceive intelligible patterns in the physical world. Words come later than things, and in *Godot* they are shown as imposing alienating preoccupations, such as Godot's arrival, that diminish our awareness of the forms that already inhere in things. It is a further tribute to the efficacy of concrete presences in *Godot* that its language recovers vitality and intensity when, adopting the techniques of metaphor and metonymy, it imitates the processes of condensation and displacement already at work in the visual form of the play. In this way, the exhaustion of thinking, so often conveyed in *Godot* by verbal language, is continuously belied by the material language of the play, which offers the possibility of a return to preverbal origins.

These concrete poetic patterns communicate to us directly, without depending on a preliminary stage in which we acquire knowledge of vocabulary and syntactical rules. They form a natural as opposed to a cultural language. The words of *Godot,* and the alienating ideas that they so frequently serve, can be understood only by someone who has been alienated by the acquisition of a language. A spectator who does not understand the language in which the play is being performed is spared a good deal of tedium because he does not fall victim to futile expectations. The play does not, however, become for him merely an incoherent jumble. Quite the contrary, he perceives an orderly pattern of relationships, based on resemblance and contiguity, that provoke an aesthetic pleasure akin to the one that is created by geometrical patterns in the play.

Finally, the promotion of relationships based on metaphor and metonomy in *Godot* also serves to undermine the law of contradiction, whose pervasive dissolution in the play was discussed in the chapter on truth. Metaphor does not simply assert the identity of two distinct things. More important, it creates a new kind of statement that attacks the distinction between "is" and "is not." To say that the day is nearing the end of its repertory implies a comparison between two terms, but it also amounts to a contradictory proposition. While inviting us to imagine ways in which "repertory" may be predicated of "day," it does not diminish our contrary awareness that they are nonetheless two very different things. Any poetic comparison, in fact, can be represented as a formula according to which the statement "A equals B" must also be interpreted as meaning "A does not equal B." Ordinary forms of predication, for example the statement "*Waiting for Godot* takes place at the end of day," preserve the law of contradiction, since they either are or are not true. Metaphor and metonymy, however, by ignoring this principle, make possible the creation of relationships that return us to an original stage of perception that existed before it was formulated.

14

Repetition and Difference

The initial stage direction of *Godot* hints at the fundamental role of repetition in the play. Estragon, failing to remove his boots after a first try "*gives up, exhausted, rests, tries again*" (7). The word *again* is then repeated in the ensuing dialogue: Vladimir greets Estragon with "So there you are again" and a moment later with "Together again at last!" These repetitions introduce us to a play in which not only words but nearly every detail of movement and gesture in repeated. Few elements of the play occur only once; rather, the rule of multiple recurrences governs throughout *Godot*.

Beckett underlines his intention of making repetition one of the structuring principles of his play in his production notebook, where he gives detailed summaries of the most important repeated actions. These include cries for help, Estragon sleeping on his stone, Vladimir and Estragon going to the tree, episodes involving doubt, moments in which characters look at the sky, and others in which they forget something. The dialogue of the play is also replete with repetitions. Vladimir answers Estragon's question about yesterday by repeating it:

> *Estragon:* What did we do yesterday?
> *Vladimir:* What did we do yesterday? (10)

Vladimir "belongs to the tree."

Repetition and Difference

When examining the running sore on Lucky's neck, Vladimir repeats Estragon's remark, "It's inevitable" (17). He also twice asks Pozzo if he wants to get rid of Lucky (21). Pozzo later joins the couple to produce a repetition of both language and gesture:

> Pozzo: (*normal voice*). No matter! What was I saying. (*He ponders.*) Wait. (*Ponders.*) Well now isn't that . . . (*he raises his head.*) Help me!
>
> Estragon: Wait!
>
> Vladimir: Wait!
>
> Pozzo: Wait!
>
> *All three take off their hats simultaneously, press their hands to their foreheads, concentrate. (27)*

Characters frequently continue a conversation by repeating phrases from statements made by others. The following exchange between Vladimir and Estragon, for example, is held together by the repetition of key words:

> Vladimir: (*hurt, coldly*). May one inquire where his Highness spent the night?
>
> Estragon: In a ditch.
>
> Vladimir (*admiringly*). A ditch! Where?
>
> Estragon: (*without gesture*). Over there.
>
> Vladimir: And they didn't beat you?
>
> Estragon: Beat me? Certainly they beat me.
>
> Vladimir: The same lot as usual?
>
> Estragon: The same? I don't know. (7)

At one point, even a stage direction echoes a phrase from the dialogue:

> Estragon: Use your intelligence, can't you?
>
> *Vladimir uses his intelligence. (12)*

As we look more closely at Beckett's use of repetition in *Godot*, we discover an important distinction. Although some repetitions repeat a word or gesture exactly as it first appeared, many others introduce a significant difference. Simple repetition of the same element is illustrated by the examples already cited. It achieves its fullest expression in the celebrated exchange that has become a hallmark of the play:

> *Estragon:*   Let's go.
> *Vladimir:*   We can't.
> *Estragon:*   Why not?
> *Vladimir:*   We're waiting for Godot.
> *Estragon:*   (*despairingly*) Ah! (10)

Vladimir's admonition is repeated six times in the play, once toward the end of Act I and five times at various places in Act II. Only in its last appearance does this exchange introduce a significant variation:

> *Estragon:*   Oh yes, let's go far away from here.
> *Vladimir:*   We can't.
> *Estragon:*   Why not?
> *Vladimir:*   We have to come back tomorrow.
> *Estragon:*   What for?
> *Vladimir:*   To wait for Godot. (59)

The effects produced by these repetitions are multiple and, in certain respects, contradictory. They imprint a kind of rhythm on the play that produces a pleasurable effect at odds with the tedium that they also create. We tire of hearing the same thing and yet also enjoy it. Repetition is boring, yet rhythm, which depends on repetition for achievement of its effects, awakens sources of pleasure even when the message it conveys to the conscious mind is a despairing one.

Repetition of difference, also the basis of metaphorical statements, is a more complex and intriguing device in *Godot*. It occurs, for example, when Vladimir and Estragon, searching for equivalents for the "sound of dead voices," compare it to such disparate things as leaves, feathers, and ashes. This is a form of repetition, in that all of these objects are presumed to be in some way identical, and yet it is a repetition of an entirely different order from the examples already mentioned. Leaves, feathers, and ashes are not by any means obviously the same thing. Grasping their common features requires a certain amount of mental effort. Furthermore, even when we have understood the basis of the comparison, we remain convinced at the same time that the objects being grouped together are, nevertheless, fundamentally distinct. It is also important to notice that this repetition involving different elements provokes none of the tedium that we feel when confronted with repetitions of the same. In the latter case, the tiresomeness of hearing the same thing must be compensated for by some positive benefit: the production of a satisfying rhythm, for example. With the repetition of difference, however, no such compensation is necessary because we instinctively enjoy the discovery that repetitions can produce differences or, conversely, that different things can be perceived as repetitions of each other.

A related example of this principle occurs when Pozzo realizes that he has lost his pipe. This episode begins in straightforward fashion with Pozzo's exclamation, "What have I done with my pipe?" (23), but the four repetitions of this phrase that immediately follow introduce significant differences. Beckett refers to Pozzo's pipe twice through synonyms, once through a brand name, and once through punctuation:

> *Pozzo:*   What can I have done with that briar?
> *Estragon:* He's a scream. He's lost his dudeen.
>   *Laughs noisily.*
>
>   . . .
>
> *Pozzo:*   (*on the point of tears*). I've lost my Kapp and Peterson!
> *Estragon:* (*convulsed with merriment*). He'll be the death of me!
> *Pozzo:*   You didn't see by any chance—. (23)

The same object is referred to repeatedly in this exchange, but we are more struck by an expansion of the semantic field than by mere repetition. We take pleasure in Beckett's inventiveness and in the discovery that there are more ways of saying "pipe" than we had previously suspected.

In addition to these verbal examples, repetitions of gestures that introduce significant differences are at work in *Godot* from the opening scene of the play. Moments after Estragon first struggles with his boots, Vladimir, according to Beckett's own phrase in his production notebook, "echoes" this gesture by removing his hat. An even more emphatic analogy in which repetition coexists with difference arises when Pozzo, sitting on his stool, mirrors, yet in a distancing way, Estragon sitting on his stone.

When Estragon walks back and forth along the apron of the stage while asking the seated Pozzo for the chicken bones, he repeats, while introducing a significance difference, Vladimir's walking toward and away from the stone at the beginning of the play. In Lucky's arrival on stage with a rope tied to his neck, we recognize an analogy with Estragon's question as to whether they are "tied" to Godot. Vladimir and Estragon's circling around Lucky retraces the half-circle formed by the rope that is now lying on the stage. Lucky's offstage fall becomes, in Act II, successive falls at center stage involving all of the characters.

After lifting Lucky to his feet at the end of Act I, Vladimir and Estragon stand on either side of him, forming a visual tableau that recalls Vladimir's verbal evocation of the story of Christ and the two thieves; they then create an additional repetition of difference by crouching on either side of Pozzo and listening to his heartbeat. Vladimir's placing his cost over the shoulders of the sleeping Estragon recalls, while underlining a significant contrast, the earlier scene in which Pozzo ordered Lucky to give him his overcoat. Similarly, his care in examining Estragon's wound is a significantly altered mirroring of Pozzo's initial inspection of them, which leads to his dimissive judgment that they are human beings, "as far as one can see" (15).

The application of this technique to the visual form of *Godot* is well illustrated by two distinct variations that Beckett works on Vladimir and Estragon's argument about the biblical story of Christ and the two thieves. He stages this argument with Vladimir crouching next to the seated Estragon as their disagreement grows more violent. Shortly after, they engage in an equally heated argument, but this time standing by the tree, which Estragon has just impugned as a mere bush. Their initial argument at the stone is recalled again at the end of Act I, but in altered form, when they sit together in silence to await the coming of night.

Beckett's variations on the initial argument, first moving it to a different location then transforming it into reconciliation, exemplify the two distinct ways in which he uses the repetition of difference to organize the scenic space of *Godot*. On the one hand, an area of the stage is the repeated setting of episodes having different connotations; each later use of this space acquires significance by recalling earlier episiodes for which it served as the setting. On the other hand, the same gesture or dialogue is moved to different parts of the stage, in which case the effect of sameness is counterbalanced by the change of place.

The technique of investing the same space with varying significance applies to Vladimir and Estragon's repeated returns to the tree. In the first of these, they argue about whether it really marks the spot of their meeting with Godot. A moment later, they are contemplating the possibility of suicide:

Vladimir: (*Silence. Estragon looks attentively at the tree.*) What do we do now?

Estragon: Wait.

Vladimir: Yes, but while waiting.

Estragon: What about hanging ourselves? (12)

The tree, which began as a simple landmark associated with an expected meeting, is suddenly transformed into a potential instrument of suicide; it is the same tree yet seen from an altered perspective. At the beginning of the second act, it acquires yet another significance when Vladimir notices that it is not quite the same tree that they last saw: "But yesterday evening it was all black and bare. And now it's covered with leaves" (42). We see the tree from an additional perspective when Vladimir and Estragon try unsuccessfully to hide behind it, leading Vladimir to observe, "Decidedly this tree will not have been the slightest use to us" (48).

The interplay between repetition and difference also arises toward the beginning of Act II when Vladimir examines Estragon's leg and helps him put on a pair of shoes. Beckett limits physical movement, once again, to the horizontal line that joins Estragon's stone to the spot where Pozzo had placed his stool. This constraint echoes the beginning of Act I, where Estragon sits on his stone and Vladimir moves back and forth along the apron of the stage. However, although this repetition is perceptible, it is by no means self-evident and not at all tedious. In Act I the spot where Vladimir comes to a halt is an empty space having no particular associations for us, except perhaps that of being distant from the stone. By the beginning of the second act, however, this spot has become strongly associated with Pozzo because this is where he sits for so long on his stool in Act I. Our response to the present scene is deepened if we recognize that Vladimir is expressing concern for Estragon, while standing in a place associated with Pozzo, who was perfectly indifferent to the sufferings of his servant in Act I. This same spot is the setting, toward the end of the play, of Vladimir's moving soliloquy beginning "Was I sleeping" (58).

Just as he invests the three points occupied by stone, tree, and stool with varying connotations, so also Beckett will make the center of the stage a setting in which to elaborate relationships based on the repetition of difference. This spot is occupied by a series of entertainers, each having his own distinct "act": Pozzo with his speech about night, Lucky with his monologue, Vladimir with his song about the dog killed by the cook, and Vladimir and Estragon with the "skit" in which they exchange hats. An even more interesting repetition occurs when Godot's messenger appears. After a brief hesitation, he walks directly to the center of the stage, where he remains throughout his appearance. His occupancy of this position automatically establishes a spatial connection between himself and Lucky, who also stood on this spot for a significant period of time. We discern a certain logic in this analogy because both Lucky and the boy are servants. But recognition of this similarity leads to acknowledgment of a corresponding difference: although Lucky's master accompanies him on stage, Godot never appears.

The repetition of movement or dialogue at different parts of the stage occurs in connection with Vladimir and Estragon's decision to leave the stage, followed by the stage direction "They do not move." This exchange is played at the end of the first act with both characters sitting on the stone, but at the end of the second with both of them standing beneath the tree. Likewise, Estragon's statement "Nothing to be done" is repeated in different locations. *Godot* begins with Estragon uttering this despairing affirmation while seated on his stone; later, he concludes the first phase of the play, which ends with the arrival of Pozzo and Lucky, by repeating the identical phrase, accompanied by an identical raised-arm gesture, but now standing on the spot where Pozzo is eventually to place his stool. The most famous example of the device of repeating dialogue in different locations on the stage is the "We're waiting for Godot" motif, which, according to an implicit yet rigorous rule, is repeated in a variety of places, with Vladimir and Estragon standing at different distances from each other and adopting different postures and gestures. Hence, even the most tedious verbal exchange in *Godot* acquires, if not quite novelty, at least a partial respite from sameness thanks to variations introduced into the scenic space of the play.

Similar effects are achieved on a larger scale in the relationship between the play's two acts. Vladimir announces the theme of change to Estragon shortly after the beginning of Act II:

Estragon: What do we do now, now that we are happy?

Vladimir: Wait for Godot. (*Estragon groans. Silence.*) Things have changed here since yesterday.

Estragon: And if he doesn't come.

Vladimir: (*after a moment of bewilderment*). We'll see when the time comes. (*Pause.*) I was saying that things have changed here since yesterday. (39)

The first episode of the second act appeals to our ability to recall the corresponding scene in Act I and to notice the significant departures that it introduces with respect to this initial model. In both acts our attention is focused on one character. But already we see differences: the character in question is not Estragon, who is for the moment offstage, but Vladimir, who is standing down stage center rather than sitting on the stone where we last saw him and where Estragon performed the pantomime with which the play begins. Furthermore, Vladimir is left alone on stage far longer than Estragon was at the beginning of Act I; he has time both to inspect his surroundings and to sing an amusing song before Estragon arrives. The conclusion of Act II also introduces another repetition of difference. The final exchange ("Well? Shall we go? . . . Yes, let's go") is exactly the same as the exchange at the end of the first act but is spoken by different characters.

The intermediary action of the second act offers countless examples that illustrate the pervasiveness of the principle of repetition of difference. Even if we do not notice that Pozzo and Lucky appear from the right rather than from the left, as they did in the first act, we cannot help but notice that the rope that connects them has been remarkably shortened. We notice as well that Lucky's two offstage falls in the first act have been transformed into a fall involving both himself and Pozzo at center stage. Vladimir and Estragon repeat their action of helping a fallen character to his feet, but this time it is Pozzo rather than Lucky. Vladimir also feeds Estragon, as he did in Act I, but he confused turnips and carrots the first time around, and now he gives him a black instead of a red radish.

As was suggested earlier in this chapter, the repetitions in *Godot* provoke contradictory responses. Repetitions of certain experiences can be inherently pleasurable. Hence, Vladimir is made happy by Estragon's return at the beginning of Act I: "I'm glad to see you back. I thought you were gone for ever" (7). On the other hand, the repetition of an experience can diminish rather than reinforce our enjoyment. Pozzo illustrates this principle when talking about smoking his pipe: "The second is never so sweet . . . as the first I mean" (19). Toward the beginning of Act II, Vladimir expresses the diversity of moods that repetition can induce:

Vladimir:	I missed you . . . and at the same time I was happy. Isn't that a queer thing?
Estragon:	(*shocked*). Happy?
Vladimir:	Perhaps it's not quite the right word.
Estragon:	And now?
Vladimir:	Now? . . . (*Joyous.*) There you are again . . . *Indifferent.*) There we are again . . . (*Gloomy.*) There I am again. (38)

Members of the audience invariably experience a similar contradiction. On the one hand, repetition produces an effect of routine and fatigue; we feel bored and want something different to happen. The discovery that the second act is largely a reppetition of the first may provoke extreme frustration. At the same time, we take pleasure in observing the significant differences that Beckett introduces into the general pattern of repetition. His characters are not generally aware of these differences since they largely pertain to the scenic space of the play, visible only to the spectators. We do have the advantage, denied to the actors, of being able to observe the complex spatial patterns that they establish by moving about the stage and creating variations that alleviate the tedium of the text. Like Vladimir, we are made both gloomy and joyous by the play's repetitions. In this way, we disprove experientially the law of contradiction and grant the existence of a region of experience in which enjoyment and frustration are inseparable.

Like metaphors, which are generated by the tension between similarity and dissimilarity, repetitions undermine the role of causality in *Godot*. A traditional play, organized around a central action, shows that action unfolding in time: later incidents in the play are logically connected to preceding incidents according to the schema of cause and effect. In *Godot*, however, the principal event that requires time for its realization, the arrival of Godot himself, never occurs. Time gradually loses its prestige in the sense that we expect increasingly less from it.

Repetition continues this process of liberating us from time by creating effects that, rather than depending on time for their fulfillment, largely suppress the role of temporality. When, for example, Vladimir and Estragon raise Pozzo to his feet at the end of the second act, we are reminded of the similar service that they perform for Lucky in Act I. Our memory of the first act coexists with its reenactment in the second act of the play: as we see one episode, we remember the other. But this simultaneity of memory and perception does not reinforce our awareness of the passage of time; on the contrary, it produces a kind of timeless moment in which two events that occurred at different times are brought together in one instantaneous experience. The contribution of sequential time to this experience is further reduced by the fact that the two events could be interchanged—with Pozzo being lifted in the first act and Lucky in the second—with little change in the effect that they produce. The fact that one event occurs *after* another has decidedly less importance than it would in a more traditional play. This is also true of the feeding episodes, in which the carrots and radishes could have been transposed without effecting the relationship between the two incidents.

The sense that time is passing is not, to be sure, completely excluded from the play, it is clearly implied by the leaves that appear on the tree, by the afflictions that have befallen Pozzo and Lucky, perhaps as well by a deepening sense of desperation in Act II. Temporality is, however, consigned by certain techniques of the play to a subordinate role. The frustrations and uncertainties of living in a world governed by time, the humiliating recognition that one will eventually die, are important thematic elements of *Godot*. But the principal techniques through which this subject is dramatized, including repetition and the use of geometrical and poetic figures to shape the spatial form of the play, conspire to deprive time of its domination.

15

Metatheater

The use of repetition as the play's fundamental structuring principle, along with rhythmical effects and geometrical figures created by the highly stylized movement of *Godot*, provoke pleasurable experiences that belie the more explicit theme of despair. A similar effect is achieved at those moments when the play becomes metatheatrical— that is, when it reminds us that we are observing on stage not an episode occurring in the real world but an imagined event taking place in a theater.

Godot is pervasively metatheatrical in that it breaks so many rules and frustrates our conventional expectations to such an extreme as to make us continually aware that we are watching a play and not real life. The stylized, unnatural way in which characters move about the stage further reminds us that they are actors obeying the exceptionally precise instructions of a director rather than real-life people making their own decisions. This awareness that we are in a theater rather than on "a country road" is, however, heightened at specific moments in the play. Such an effect occurs, for example, when Estragon, gazing on the audience, declares that he finds us "inspiring prospects" (10). A less flattering but equally metatheatrical appraisal occurs in Act II

Estragon "echoes" Vladimir's earlier inspection of his hat.

when Vladimir and Estragon, frightened by offstage noises, run about the stage looking for a way of escape:

> *Vladimir:* We're surrounded (*Estragon makes a rush towards back.*) Imbecile! There's no way out there. (*He takes Estragon by the arm and drags him towards front. Gesture towards front.*) There! Not a soul in sight! Off you go! Quick! (*He pushes Estragon towards the auditorium. Estragon recoils in horror.*) You won't? (*He contemplates auditorium.*) Well I can understand that. (47)

Estragon's reluctance to join us in the auditorium and Vladimir's sympathetic approval of his decision deprive us of our invisibility. In conventional plays we as spectators enjoy the sole privilege of watching, but *Godot* forces on us the recognition that we are, in turn, being watched by the actors. The theatrical illusion collapses, and we find ourselves face to face not with Vladimir and Estragon placed amid an enigmatic setting far removed from our secure vantage in the auditorium, but with actors who are playing roles and who affirm the obvious fact that they are right there with us in the theater.

At certain moments Vladimir and Estragon's remarks about the play reflect our own reactions as spectators and, in this way, create a similarly metatheatrical effect. Toward the beginning of *Godot*, Estragon tells Vladimir that he finds the latter's recounting of the story of Christ and the two thieves "really most extraordinarily interesting (9), a comment that may allude ironically to our own feelings. Vladimir and Estragon later express, again in such a way as to mirror our own responses, the experience of boredom that the play has produced:

> *Vladimir:* Charming evening we're having.
>
> *Estragon:* Unforgettable.
>
> *Vladimir* And it's not over.
>
> *Estragon:* Apparently not.
>
> *Vladimir:* It's only beginning
>
> *Estragon:* It's awful.

Vladimir: Worse than the pantomime.
Estragon: The circus.
Vladimir: The music-hall.
Estragon: The circus. (23)

Not only does this exchange transform Vladimir and Estragon into the audience of a play in which they are also the principal characters. It further conveys to us their awareness that the setting of their performance is not "real life" but a play and clearly one whose author has borrowed techniques from other traditional forms of entertainment, including pantomime, circus, and music hall.

Brief phrases from the dialogue further reinforce our awareness of the theatricality of *Godot*. Vladimir, for example, describes the day's activities in terms of a metaphor drawn from the theater: "But it is not for nothing I have lived through this long day and I can assure you it is very near the end of its repertory" (55). A metonymy creates a similar effect when Pozzo, blind and unsure of where he is in Act II, asks Vladimir: "It isn't by any chance the place known as the Board?" (55). Vladimir's disclaimer that he "never heard of it" does not diminish the momentary suspension of the theatrical illusion, whereby we recognize that they are indeed standing on boards and not on a country road.

Further reminders occur when characters on stage perform for each other. While Pozzo declaims his speech on the coming of night, or Lucky performs his dance and then recites his monologue, we recognize that Vladimir and Estragon's relationship to these performances mirrors our own relation to the play as a whole. We are, at these moments, watching a play in which certain characters are, likewise, watching a play that is being performed for them. Pozzo stresses his metatheatrical role as performer when he asks Vladimir and Estragon to comment on his monologue:

Pozzo: How did you find me? (*Vladimir and Estragon look at him blankly.*) Good? Fair? Middling? Poor? Positively bad?
Vladimir: (*first to understand*). Oh very good, very very good.

Metatheater

Pozzo: (*To Estragon*). And you, sir?

Estragon: Oh tray bong, tray tray tray bong. (25)

A moment later Estragon expresses a more honest reaction that makes us, once again, self-conscious about our own responses to the play: "Nothing happens, nobody comes, nobody goes, it's awful!" (27).

The frequent appearance of metatheatrical elements in *Godot* leads to a number of observations. In the first place, whenever such moments occur, we experience a sense of liberation. The mirroring of our own act of watching the play creates a kind of pleasure that is unmistakable even though its source may be difficult to ascertain. Although nothing is to be expected from the passage of time in the play, there are, frequently enough to make *Godot* endurable and even enjoyable, momentary ruptures in which a sudden shift in our relation to the stage replaces the merely tedious act of anticipating some future event.

One reason for our pleasure may be that these metatheatrical effects cause us to perceive the scenic space of *Godot* in a way that frees us from the rational constraints of the law of contradiction. In chapter 13 I pointed out that metaphoric statements are distinguished from ordinary logical statements by the fact that they simultaneously affirm that "A is B" and "A is not B." Metaphor, which allows positive and negative statements to coexist, violates in this way the foundation of rational thinking, an act that produces both disorienting and pleasurable effects.

This peaceful coexistence of "is/is not" statements is also an inherent aspect of theatrical space. Whenever we watch a play we automatically "suspend our disbelief" by assuming that the actors really are the characters they pretend to be. Likewise, we accept the illusion that the stage is a palace, or someone's living room, or a country road, that characters are saying things that are inspired by their situation, that they do not know what is going to happen next, and so forth. Briefly, we acquiesce in the assumption that the fictional world of the play really exists. However, we know at the same time that this is not true. The stage is a platform that has been built in a theater, and the characters are really actors who have memorized the lines that they seem spontaneously to utter and who know what is happening and going to happen at every instant of the play. In *Godot* they unmistakably know precisely what movements and gestures are expected of them.

Whenever we watch a play we implicitly accept the logical contradiction of believing that something is true even though we know that it is not. The difference between conventional drama and a highly metatheatrical play such as *Godot* is that the former tends to suppress the contradiction, whereas the latter pushes our awareness of it to an extreme limit. Being made aware of that contradiction between belief and disbelief implied by our participation in the theatrical act is a pleasurable experience probably because, as in the case of metaphor and metonomy, it restores in waking experience the ambiguity that had been banished by the establishment of rational structures. From one point of view the play tantalizes us with such questions as whether Godot is coming or not, whether the act of waiting is or is not deserving of our approval, and so forth. All of these questions, however, based on the assumption of a clear distinction between affirmation and negation, are posed in the context of a play that continually points to the dissolution of any such stable boundary.

In chapter 12 I called attention to the fact that the scenic space of *Godot* is decentered. Our attention is first deflected from the center of the stage by the diagonal line running from the stone to the tree, an effect that is deepened by the fact that the main characters tend to adopt off-center positions. Metatheatrical devices contribute to this effect by disturbing the unity of the stage in *Godot* in such a way as to confer on it a double, contradictory identity, as both stage and country road. We perceive the stage as two different and, from the rational point of view, irreconcilable things. An analogous kind of splitting occurs when characters perform for each other, an act that divides the stage into two spaces, one occupied by the performer, the other by his spectators. Some of *Godot's* "real" spectators may even feel that the auditorium, made self-consciously visible by the metatheatrical games of the play, becomes itself a third term that creates a triangular space. The unity of the scenic space is further diminished by the fact that

Godot borrows from so many different theatrical traditions: one moment we are watching a religious drama, then a vaudeville show, then a circus act. This shift from one form to another introduces additional displacements into our perception of the theatrical space.

Although the text of the play continually turns our attention to the presumed centrality of Godot, the lack of center on the stage itself and the more subtle kind of decentering created by metatheatrical moments in the play give no material support to this notion of a privileged center. The belief in its existence is merely a mental representation constructed in obvious defiance of the physical evidence.

The presence of metatheatrical elements in *Godot* shifts our attention away from representation, from what characters are pretending to be doing, and toward the purely theatrical quality of their performance. If these devices did not exist we would have good reason to think that the play was essentially intended to represent a certain range of human experiences—to portray, for example, the act of waiting or the master/slave relationship. Just as physical movement replaces dramatic action in *Godot,* however, so also the act of performing a play takes precedence over any external reality to which it may refer. This shift from representation to enactment should remind us that although Beckett is notoriously indifferent to presumed meanings, he has expended considerable energy on actual productions of his plays. His indifference to what the play represents coexists with the most intense concern with the way in which it is performed.

Finally, *Godot* is metatheatrical in the sense that it reflects on the circumstances of its own creation. Beckett traces the inception of *Godot* to its origins in human desire while implicitly contrasting the creation of an artistic work with other paths that desire may follow. Normally, desire tends toward satisfaction; it searches for objects that will give it the fulfillment and release that it seeks. The desire that culminates in a work of art, on the contrary, aims not at satisfaction but at self-delight, the pleasure in its own existence, which it seeks to cultivate and prolong.

Sigmund Freud has made the useful suggestion that desire may follow three distinct paths: neurosis, perversion, and sublimation. Neurotic desire suffers from inhibitions that make satisfaction impossible and create substitute forms of symptomatic behavior. Perverse desire ignores the barriers that create inhibitions; rather than allowing itself to be molded by approved norms, it pursues the direct, unrestrained satisfaction of instincts that civilized adults are expected to have renounced. The third alternative, sublimation, allows the artist to pursue those instinctual satisfactions that are blocked by neurosis but in such a way as to recognize the prerogatives of civilized life. Rather than remaining fixated at the level of infantile forms of direct satisfaction such as are pursued in perversion, the artist creates something whose social value is recognized and legitimated. In this way, he satisfies infantile impulses while avoiding mere regression. Freud's model is useful in part because it allows us to treat the pervasive motifs of impotence and sadomasochism in *Godot* in a metatheatrical way. In other words, rather than wondering whether these pathologies reflect the author's personal difficulties or his vision of contemporary society, we can interpret them as expressing unsatisfactory outcomes of desire, which we may then contrast with the sublimated outcome that is the play itself.

Inhibition is chiefly represented in the play by Vladimir, who frequently prevents Estragon from acting on his impulses, principally among them the spontaneous wish to leave the stage. Similarly, Vladimir refuses to listen to Estragon's dreams, suggesting his indifference to the instinctual life that they reveal. Neurosis is further suggested by Vladimir's affirmation that the range of prohibited desires is extremely large, extending even to include an interdiction against laughter (8), and by his fear that Godot will punish them if they do not continue their vigil (59). It is appropriate, given his censoring function, that Vladimir should initiate a conversation with Estragon by suggesting, "What if we repent?," and equally appropriate that Estragon does not understand the relevance of repentance to themselves.

Pozzo, on the other hand, is largely free of the inhibitions that afflict Vladimir. He pursues direct and uninhibited satisfaction of those desires that the two main characters can express only timidly and with little prospect of real satisfaction. Pozzo has organized life in such a way as to assure maximum gratification of his instinctual needs and seems not at all aware of the sorts of considerations—respectability, propriety, fear of punishment—that weigh so heavily on Vladimir. He has no idea who Godot is and, consequently, feels no temptation to defer immediate satisfaction of his impulses in the hope that some superior form of satisfaction will eventually be granted him. With Pozzo the passage from impulse to action is direct and immediate: he eats voraciously, guzzles his wine, beats his servant, belches, and shouts to gain attention with a complete lack of inhibition.

Interpretations of *Godot* suggesting that the moral center of the work lies in the choice between the two couples are reductive in the sense that they limit us to a choice between neurosis and perversion. For the artist, however, the third alternative of sublimation is equally available, as it is to his audience. The pleasure that we experience in responding to the aesthetic features of *Godot* is sublimated, in contrast to the neurotic and perverse evolutions of desire that we see exemplified by the two couples. Sublimation is a solution to the problem of neurosis in the sense that it recognizes the legitimacy of instinct, when it awakens and draws out rather than prohibits. Likewise, it escapes the limits of perversion because the object that it proposes is not an infantile object, which grants only temporary instinctual satisfaction, but a highly evolved, cultural object, which unfailingly renews instinctual life because its turns us away from the quest for satisfaction and toward delight in its own existence.

To say that the sublimated enjoyments that *Godot* offers are preferable to the paths pursued by the two couples is not to offer an essentially moral judgment. Sublimated enjoyments are superior because they gratify instincts that are denied by neurosis and doomed to unsatisfactory fulfillments by perversion. Unlike Godot, who will never come, and Pozzo and Lucky, in whose arrivals and departures we behold the pursuit of evanescent satisfactions, *Godot* itself will never disappear.

Notes

1. "Dante . . . Bruno . Vico . . Joyce," in *Our Exagmination Round His Factification for Incamination of Work in Progress* (Paris: Shakespeare & Co., 1929), 3–22.

2. *Proust* (New York: Grove Press, 1957).

3. Antonin Artaud, *The Theater and Its Double* (New York: Grove Press, (1958).

4. "*En Attendant Godot,*" in Roger Blin, *Souvenirs et Propos* ed. Lynda Bellity Peskine (Paris: Gallimard, 1986), 80–105.

5. Sigmund Freud, "Moses and Monotheism," in *The Standard Edition of the Complete Psychological Works,* trans. James Strachey (London: Hogarth Press, 1964), 23:7–137.

6. Alan Schneider, "Working with Beckett," in *Samuel Beckett: The Critical Heritage,* ed. Lawrence Graver and Raymond Federman (London, Henley, and Boston: Routledge & Kegan Paul, 1979), 173–88.

7. In Graver and Federman, *Samuel Beckett,* 97–104.

8. Hélène L. Baldwin, *Samuel Beckett's Real Silence* (University Park and London: Pennsylvania State University Press, 1981).

9. Nathan Scott, *Samuel Beckett* (New York: Hillary House, 1965).

10. Bert States, *The Shape of Paradox* (Berkeley: University of California Press, 1978).

11. Curtis Brooks, "The Mythic Pattern in *Waiting for Godot,*" *Modern Drama* 9 (1966): 292–99.

12. Lois Cuddy, "Beckett's 'Dead Voices' in *Waiting for Godot:* New Inhabitants of Dante's *Inferno,*" *Modern Language Studies* 12, no. 2 (1982): 48–61.

13. David Hesla, *The Shape of Chaos: An Interpretation of the Art of Samuel Beckett* (Minneapolis: University of Minnesota Press, 1971).

14. Dan O. Via, Jr., "*Waiting for Godot* and Man's Search for Community," *Journal of Bible and Religion* (January 1962): 32–37.

15. Hugh Kenner, *Samuel Beckett: A Critical Study* (New York: Grove Press, 1961), 132.

16. Darko Suvin, "Preparing for Godot—or the Purgatory of Individualism," in *Casebook on "Waiting for Godot,"* ed. Ruby Cohn (New York: Grove Press, 1967), 121–32.

17. Gabor Mihalyi, "Beckett's *Godot* and the Myth of Alienation," *Modern Drama* 9 (1966): 277–82.

18. John Fletcher, *Samuel Beckett's Art* (London: Chatto & Windus, 1967).

19. Martin Esslin, *The Theater of the Absurd* (New York: Anchor Books, 1969).

20. Eugene Webb, *The Plays of Samuel Beckett.* (Seattle: University of Washington Press, 1972).

21. Gunther Anders, "Being without Time," in *Samuel Beckett,* ed. Martin Esslin (Englewood Cliffs, N.J.: Prentice-Hall, 1965), 140–51.

22. In Graver and Federman, *Samuel Beckett,* 95–97.

23. Blin, *Souvenirs et Propos,* 95.

24. In Graver and Federman, *Samuel Beckett,* 115.

25. Deirdre Bair, *Samuel Beckett: A Biography* (New York and London: Harcourt Brace Jovanovich, 1978), 637.

26. In Graver and Federman, *Samuel Beckett,* 89–92.

27. Ibid., 93–95.

28. Alan Schneider, *Entrances: An American Director's Journey* (New York: Viking, 1986).

29. John Fletcher and John Spurling, *Beckett the Playwright* (London: Methuen, 1985), 64.

30. Mihalyi, "Beckett's *Godot,*" 278.

31. Fletcher and Spurling, *Beckett the Playwright,* 65

32. Ruby Cohn, "The Churn of Stale Words: Repetitions," in *Just Play: Beckett's Theater* (Princeton, N.J.: Princeton University Press, 1980), 96–107.

33. Dougald McMillan and Martha Fehsenfeld, *Beckett in Theater* (London: John Calder; New York: Riverrun Press, 1988).

34. Dina Scherzer, "Deconstruction in *Waiting for Godot,*" in *The Reversible World: Symbolic Inversion in Art and Society,* ed. Barbara A. Babcock (Ithaca, N.Y.: Cornell University Press, 1978).

35. Aspasia Velissariou, "Language in *Waiting for Godot,*" *Journal of Beckett Studies* 8 (1982): 45–57.

36. Pierre Chabert, "The Body in Beckett's Theater," *Journal of Beckett Studies* 8 (1982): 23–28.

37. Bair, *Samuel Beckett,* 18.

Notes

38. Blin, *Souvenirs et Propos*, 85–86.
39. *Proust*, 11.
40. Ibid., 29–30.
41. Ibid., 14.
42. Ibid., 22–23.
43. Ibid., 63.
44. Ibid., 32.
45. Walter D. Asmus, "A Rehearsal Diary," in *Beckett in Theater*, 137.

Bibliography

Primary Works

Collected Poems in English in French. New York: Grove Press, 1977.
The Collected Shorter Plays of Samuel Beckett. New York: Grove Press, 1984.
Company. New York: Grove Press, 1980.
Endgame. New York: Grove Press, 1958.
Film. New York: Grove Press, 1969.
Fizzles. New York: Grove Press, 1976.
First Love and Other Shorts. New York: Grove Press, 1974.
Happy Days. New York: Grove Press, 1961.
How It Is. New York: Grove Press, 1964.
Krapp's Last Tape and Other Dramatic Pieces. New York: Grove Press, 1960.
The Lost Ones. New York: Grove Press, 1972.
Mercier and Camier. New York: Grove Press, 1974.
More Pricks Than Kicks. New York: Grove Press, 1972
Murphy. New York: Grove Press, 1957.
Proust. New York: Grove Press, 1957.
Stories and Texts for Nothing. New York: Grove Press, 1965.
Three Novels (Molloy, Malone Dies, The Unnamable). New York: Grove
    Press, 1965.
Waiting for Godot. New York: Grove Press, 1954.
Watt. New York: Grove Press, 1959.

Secondary Works

Books

Baldwin, Hélène L. *Samuel Beckett's Real Silence.* University Park and Lon-
    don: Pennsylvania State University Press, 1981. Christian interpretation
    of *Godot* in terms of mystical experience of God's absence.

Bibliography

Bair, Deirdre. *Samuel Beckett: A Biography.* New York and London: Harcourt Brace Jovanovich, 1978. Biographical context of *Godot.*

Bloom, Harold, ed. *Samuel Beckett's "Waiting for Godot."* Modern Critical Interpretations. New York: Chelsea House Publishers, 1987. Collection of critical essays.

Brater, Enoch. *Beckett at 80/Beckett in Context.* New York: Oxford University Press, 1986. Essays in celebration of Beckett's eightieth birthday, including several by scholars who first encountered *Godot* in the 1950s.

Busi, Frederick. *The Transformations of "Godot."* Lexington: University of Kentucky Press, 1980. Analysis of proper names in relation to major themes of play.

Cohn, Ruby. *Samuel Beckett: The Comic Gamut.* New Brunswick, N.J.: Rutgers University Press, 1962. Beckett's use of comic devices; allusions to Christianity.

————. *Casebook on "Waiting for Godot."* New York: Grove Press, 1967. Original reviews of the play and interpretive essays.

————. *Just Play: Beckett's Theater.* Princeton, N.J.: Princeton University Press, 1980. Extended discussion of repetition in *Godot.*

————, ed. *Beckett: "Waiting for Godot."* Casebook Series. London: MacMillan Education Ltd., 1987. A collection of reviews and critical articles, including several on recent productions of *Godot.*

Cormier, Ramona, and Janis Pallister. *Waiting for Death: The Philosophical Significance of Beckett's "Waiting for Godot."* University: University of Alabama Press, 1979. *Godot* as a dramatization of absurdity and human finitude. Beckett's relation to contemporary philosophers.

Esslin, Martin. *The Theater of the Absurd.* New York: Anchor Books, 1969. *Godot* as absurdist drama.

Fletcher, John, and Beryl Fletcher. *A Student's Guide to the Plays of Samuel Beckett.* London: Faber & Faber, 1985. Useful introduction to *Godot* as well as notes on the text of the play.

Fletcher, John, and John Spurling. *Beckett the Playwright.* London: Methuen, 1985. Contribution of repetition to the "shape" of *Godot.*

Graver, Lawrence, and Raymond Federman, eds. *Samuel Beckett: The Critical Heritage.* London, Henley, and Boston: Routledge & Kegan Paul, 1979. Reviews of the first productions of *Godot.*

Hesla, David. *The Shape of Chaos: An Interpretation of the Art of Samuel Beckett.* Minneapolis: University of Minnesota Press, 1971. Analysis of *Godot* employing ideas of German philosopher Martin Heidegger.

Kenner, Hugh. *A Reader's Guide to Samuel Beckett.* New York: Farrar, Straus & Giroux, 1973. *Godot* as self-contained, highly symmetrical dramatization of experience of waiting; sources in Laurel and Hardy.

Knowlson, James, and Dougald McMillan, eds. *The Theatrical Notebooks of Sameul Beckett*, vol. 1: *Waiting for Godot*, with a revised text. London: Faber & Faber; New York: Grove Press, forthcoming. Facsimile edition of Beckett's directorial notebooks for 1975 Schiller Theater production; the revised text of *Godot* is approved by Beckett.

McMillan, Dougald, and Martha Fehsenfeld, *Beckett in Theater*. London: John Calder; New York: Riverrun Press, 1988. Analysis of Beckett's notebooks for 1975 production of *Godot* and comprehensive collection of his commentary on the play.

Schneider, Alan. *Entrances: An American Director's Journey*. New York: Viking, 1986. Recollections of his first encounter with *Godot* and conversations with Beckett about the play, by his American director.

States, Bert. *The Shape of Paradox*. Berkeley: University of California Press, 1978. Sees *Godot* as an accommodation of the biblical theme of man after the Fall to the contemporary experience of despair and alienation.

Webb, Eugene. *The Plays of Samuel Beckett*. Seattle: University of Washington Press, 1972. Argues that *Godot* illustrates the breakdown of discredited patterns of thought and belief.

Articles

Anders, Gunther. "Being without Time: On Beckett's Play *Waiting for Godot*." In *Samuel Beckett: A Collection of Critical Essays*, edited by Martin Esslin, 140–51. Englewood Cliffs, N.J.: Prentice-Hall, 1965. *Godot* illustrates man's inability to embrace nihilism.

Asmus, Walter D. "A Rehearsal Diary." In *Beckett in Theater*, edited by Dougald McMillan and Martha Fehsenfeld, 136–47. London: John Calder; New York: Riverrun Press, 1988. Details of Beckett's direction of the 1975 Schiller Theater production of *Godot* as noted by his assistant director.

Brooks, Curtis. "The Mythic Pattern in *Waiting for Godot*." *Modern Drama* 9 (1966):292–99. Connections between *Godot* and ancient ritual; disappearance of maternal figure.

Chabert, Pierre. "The Body in Beckett's Theater." *Journal of Beckett Studies* 8 (1982):23–28. Beckett's liberation of the body from traditional subservience to meaning.

Cuddy, Lois. "Beckett's 'Dead Voices' in *Waiting for Godot:* New Inhabitants of Dante's *Inferno*." *Modern Language Studies* 12, no. 2 (1982):48–61. *Godot* as a modern reworking of the third canto of Dante's *Inferno*.

Duckworth, Colin. "The Making of *Godot*." In *Casebook on "Waiting for Godot,"* edited by Ruby Cohn, 89–100. Sources of *Godot* in Beckett's novella *Mercier and Camier*.

Bibliography

————. "Beckett's New *Godot*." In *Beckett's Later Fiction and Drama: Texts for Company*, edited by James Acheson and Kateryna Arthur, 175–92. New York: St. Martin's Press, 1987. Analysis of Beckett's 1984 production of *Godot* with the San Quentin Drama Workshop, including an interview with the actors.

Esslin, Martin. "Towards the Zero of Language." In James Acheson and Katerina Arthur, *Beckett's Later Fiction*, 35–49. New York: St. Martin's Press, 1987. Decreasing importance of language in Beckett's work.

Gans, Eric. "Beckett and the Problem of Modern Culture." *Substance* 35 (1982):3–15. An analysis of *Godot's* broader historical significance.

Iser, Wolfgang. "The Art of Failure: The Stifled Laugh in Beckett's Theater." *Bucknell Review* 26, no. 1 (1978): 139–89. The hesitant laughter provoked by Beckett's plays arises from conflict between desire for liberation from repressive constraints and fear of losing the security they provide.

Knowlson, James. "Beckett as Director: The Manuscript Production Notebooks and Critical Interpretation." *Modern Drama* 30, no. 4 (1987): 451–65. Study of Beckett's approach to directing his plays illuminates our understanding of them.

Metman, Eva. "Reflections on Samuel Beckett's Plays." In *Samuel Beckett*, edited by Martin Esslin, 117–39. Englewood Cliffs, N.J.: Prentice-Hall, 1965. Jungian interpretation of *Godot* in relation to problems of modern culture. Godot's function is to keep men unconscious.

Mihalyi, Gabor. "Beckett's *Godot* and the Myth of Alienation." *Modern Drama* 9 (1966): 277–82. By destroying old and no longer credible myths *Godot* prepares the way for human renewal.

Robbe-Grillet, Alain. "Samuel Beckett, or Presence on the Stage." In *For a New Novel*, trans. Richard Howard. New York: Grove Press, 1965. Contends that the function of Vladimir and Estragon, beyond any abstract interpretations they may inspire, is simply to be *present* on stage.

Scherzer, Dina. "Deconstruction in *Waiting for Godot*." In *The Reversible World: Symbolic Inversion in Art and Society*, edited by Barbara A. Babcock, 129–46. Ithaca, N.Y.: Cornell University Press, 1978. Comprehensive analysis of devices used in dialogue to undermine meaning and to promote playfulness of language.

Velissariou, Aspasia. "Language in *Waiting for Godot*." *Journal of Beckett Studies* 8 (1982):45–57. Beckett subverts the imperialism of language, which alienates us from our real selves.

Via, Dan O., Jr. "*Waiting for Godot* and Man's Search for Community." *Journal of Bible and Religion* (January 1962):32–37. Vladimir and Estragon long for community but are unwilling to become available to each other.

INDEX

Anders, Gunther, 15
Antigone, 79
Apollinaire, Guillaume, 2
Aristotle, 53–54, 60, 79
Artaud, Antonin, 3–4
Asmus, Walter, 97

Bair, Deirdre, 16
Baldwin, Hélène, 11
Beckett, Samuel
  Comments on *Godot:* 4, 11, 25,
    55, 80, 89, 97, 105, 123
  WORKS
  ESSAYS: *Proust,* 1, 53, 61, 64, 71–
    72, 77
  FICTION: *Molloy,* 80; *Murphy,* 4;
    Watt, 84
  PLAYS: "Eleutheria," 79;
    Endgame, 4, 38; *Happy Days,*
    4; *Not I,* 4; *Play,* 4; *Rockaby,* 4
  POETRY: *Whoroscope,* 44
Blin, Roger, 4, 10, 16, 25
Breton, André, 3
Brooks, Curtis, 12
Buber, Martin, 13

Causality, 23, 53–61, 115
Chabert, Pierre, 18
Christianity, 11, 21, 23, 25–31, 46
Cluchey, Rich, 6
Cohn, Ruby, 17

Copernicus, Nicholas, 8
Cuddy, Lois, 13

Dante, 13
Derrida, Jacques, 18
Descartes, René, 21, 22, 24, 34–35,
  36, 41–42
Dreaming, 13, 39–40, 57, 74–78

Esslin, Martin, 14
Ethical dimension, 12–14, 18, 31,
  71, 118–19

Fletcher, John, 14, 36; and John
  Spurling, 17
Fraser, G.S., 11
Freud, Sigmund, 8, 27, 123

Hall, Peter, 15
Hamlet, 7
Hesla, David, 13
Hobson, Harold, 16

Jouve, Pierre-Jean, 1
Joyce, James, 1–2, 85

Kenner, Hugh, 13
King Lear, 79

Language, 3, 4, 7, 17, 18, 22, 23, 43–
  52, 83, 85–86, 96, 103–104

Law of contradiction, 36–39, 104, 121
Lemarchand, Jacques, 16

Macabru, Pierre, 16
McMillan, Dougald, and Martha Fehsenfeld, 17
Maternal figure, 8–9, 28–29, 80, 82
Meaning, 3–5, 7, 11, 12, 15–18, 25, 27, 51–52, 86–87, 93–95, 97, 123
Memory and expectation, 2, 11–12, 13–15, 24, 26, 27–30, 33, 45, 62–69, 84, 89, 94, 103–104, 115–16, 121
Metaphor and metonymy, 5, 45, 97–104, 108, 115, 120–22
Mihalyi, Gabor, 14, 17
Mother Courage, 79

Nietzsche, Friedrich, 6

Oedipus Rex, 79

Patriarchy, 8–9, 12, 82–83

Rationality, 2–3, 8, 22, 37–42, 122
Repetition and difference, 5, 7, 51–52, 61, 105–16

Repression, 18, 22, 31, 43–46, 52, 64, 75–77, 87, 124–25

San Quentin Drama Workshop, 6
Scherzer, Dina, 18
Schiller Theater production, 3, 7, 15, 16, 17, 55, 97
Schneider, Alan, 11, 17, 97
Schopenhauer, Arthur, 14, 30
Scott, Nathan, 11–12
Six Characters in Search of an Author, 79
States, Bert, 12
Strindberg, August, 10
Sublimation, 123–25
Surrealism, 2–3
Suvin, Darko, 14

Theater of the absurd, 14–15
Truth, 22, 23, 27, 32–42, 73–78
Tynan, Kenneth, 15

Velissariou, Aspasia, 18
Via, Dan O., 13
Visual Form, 3–5, 7, 15–17, 23–24, 49, 68, 86–87, 89–96, 97–98, 100–103, 110–15

Webb, Eugene, 15

Yeats, William Butler, 31

ABOUT THE AUTHOR

Thomas Cousineau is associate professor of English at Washington College in Chestertown, Maryland. A graduate of Boston College and the University of California at Davis, he began his teaching career as visiting professor of English at the University of Lille and has returned to teach in French universities on several occasions. His articles on Beckett have appeared in *Modern Fiction Studies, Journal of Beckett Studies, College Literature,* and *Southern Humanities Review.* This study is based on a seminar he was invited to teach at the Sorbonne and Nanterre campuses of the University of Paris.